BUDGERIGARS

1 ... now-
l(... wco-
n ... eed-
ir ... here
is ... st to
the experienced.

Cyril Rogers covers the subject completely and concisely, with special regard for the buying of stock, housing, feeding, colour breeding and ailments.

BUDGERIGARS

BY

CYRIL H. ROGERS, F.B.S.A.

Revised Edition

FOYLES HANDBOOKS
LONDON

ISBN 0 7071 0609 5

© *W. & G. Foyle Ltd. 1960*

Reprinted 1968
Reprinted 1970
Revised edition 1973
Reprinted 1976
Reprinted 1977
Reprinted 1978
Reprinted 1979
Reprinted 1981
Reprinted 1982
Reprinted 1983
Reprinted 1984
Reprinted 1985
Reprinted 1986
Reprinted 1989

Published in Great Britain by
W. & G. Foyle Ltd.,
125 Charing Cross Road,
London, WC2H 0EB

Printed and bound in Great Britain
at The Bath Press, Avon

CONTENTS

INTRODUCTION

THIS Handbook has been written with the primary object of assisting the many newcomers to the delightful hobby of breeding and keeping Budgerigars. Certain features of a more technical nature have been explained in, I hope, a manner that will be easily understood by all. The more advanced breeders are asked to overlook any divergence from strict technical details which may have been used for the sake of simplicity. It has not been possible to give coloured Plates because of the very high cost, but I have endeavoured to convey in words the beauties of the colouring of the many and varied types. If the colour descriptions are read together with reference to the Plates a very good picture of the various colours can be ascertained. It is hoped that this book will help those who have recently acquired Budgerigars and also introduce these charming birds to a larger range of the bird loving public.

CYRIL H. ROGERS.

CHAPTER 1

HISTORY

1. FIRST IMPORTATION

It was not until the year 1840 that the renowned Naturalist Gould brought to Britain the first wild-caught Australian Light Green Budgerigars. Their very pleasing behaviour, both in cage and aviary, quickly made them popular with bird keepers both here and on the Continent of Europe. In the past they have been known by a variety of names such as Undulated Parrakeets, Zebra Parrakeets, Warbling Parrakeets, etc. The universal name of to-day, 'Budgerigar', is a corruption of an Australian Aboriginal name meaning 'Pretty Bird'.

2. HABITAT

Budgerigars in their wild state inhabit large tracts of country in the wild grassy plains of Australia. Their natural wild colouring is light green: however, mutations or 'sports' do happen in the wild flocks and Naturalists have reported from time to time seeing yellow and even blue coloured Budgerigars flying wild with the huge flocks of green ones. Odd specimens of Opaline, Cinnamon and Dark Green have also been recorded as wild-caught.

3. FIRST MUTATIONS

For the first twenty-five to thirty years Light Green Budgerigars were breeding freely in Britain, all true to their wild colour, but during the early 1870s a Yellow mutation occurred. A few years prior to this two Yellow mutations had appeared on the Continent, one type like the British form and the other being pure yellow with red eyes. Unfortunately these first red-eyed Yellows were not established and the mutation did not appear again until many years later. Several strains of the normal dark

eyed Yellows were founded and from them have descended the
Light Yellows of the present time.

4. LIGHT BLUES (SKY BLUES) APPEAR

About ten years after the Yellows had been established a Light
Blue mutation occurred in Europe and was carefully preserved
and established. However, it was not until the year 1910 that the
first Blue Budgerigars were seen in this country and they certainly caused a big sensation in the bird world by their delicate
and unusual colouring. They were first exhibited by R. Pauwels
at the Crystal Palace Show, London.

5. THE DARK VARIETY

In 1915, again on the Continent, the next colour variation, the
Laurel Green, occurred. This mutation was really a series of
colours and these Laurel Greens also gave rise to three other
shades. The Laurel Greens, or as we now call them Dark Greens,
were produced in the huge Budgerigar breeding establishment of
Mon. A. Blanchard of Toulouse, France. The following year Olive Greens were bred from the 'Laurels' and then the first cross
breeding experiments were started. Light Blues were crossed
with Olive Greens producing the first known 'Blue bred' Laurel
Greens. By the pairing together of such Laurel Green birds and
also by crossing them back to Light Blues the first Cobalts, or
Powder Blues to give them one of their original names, were
evolved in 1920. The Mauves which were quickly produced from
the Cobalt birds were of a much more pleasing shade of colour
than the mauve birds we see to-day, so much so in fact that they
were invariably called 'Lavenders'.

6. APPLE GREENS (GREYWING GREENS)

The exact date or the place where the first Greywing Greens
occurred have not been accurately recorded but it is known
that mutations appeared several times between 1918 and 1925
both in France and Britain. Greywing Greens were originally
called Apple Greens, Satinettes, or Jades according to the
depth of their body colour and the Greywing Blues were
known as Silverwings. It was through this confusion of names

for this handsomely coloured variety that a Colour Committee was formed by the Budgerigar Club to name and classify new coloured birds as and when they appeared.

7. COLOURS IN PROFUSION

Before the Greywings had really fully established themselves as favourites in breeding aviaries and in the exhibitions a whole spate of new and exciting colours made their appearance and caused the Greywings to take a back seat. During the early part of 1931 the first Cinnamon (Cinnamonwing) mutation occurred in Britain followed closely by two more, one in Australia and the other in Germany. In addition to being a new colour the Cinnamon was also the first of the sex-linked characters and opened up new fields of experimental breeding in the Budgerigar Fancy. Also in 1931 another unusual mutant appeared, this time on the other side of the world where in California the red-eyed Fallows in their green and yellow forms were bred but unfortunately this mutation was not fixed. The loss of the Californian mutation was fortunately not a very serious setback as during the following season an identical Fallow mutation was bred in Germany. These German Fallows were quickly established in a whole range of colours and a number were imported into Britain where for a time they were very popular with breeders and exhibitors. Other Fallow mutations have occurred in such widely separated places as Australia, South Africa and the U.S.A. Another Fallow type was produced in Britain during the early 1930s and although similar in all respects to the German form it owed its colour characteristics to quite a different set of hereditary characters. During the same period a race of birds with highly coloured plumage and having plum coloured eyes were produced and established in Britain. Although interesting from a breeding point of view these plum eyed birds were not very striking in colour and unfortunately during the 1939–45 war the strain was apparently lost.

8. A NEW DOMINANT

For some time a violet coloured variety was in existence in Britain but much doubt existed as to their breeding behaviour and the strain was difficult to preserve. Fortunately enough, a further violet mutation was recorded in Australia and these birds were of a Dominant kind. The Australian Dominant Violet was introduced into this country and from them many lovely coloured violet types have been produced.

9. ALBINOS AND LUTINOS

Following closely on the heels of the Fallows came the Albinos and Lutinos in their sex-linked form, again being first produced on the Continent, although an Albino was bred in Britain at about the same time but died without issue. A further red-eyed mutation appeared in Britain during 1936, this time the Lutino kind from which a race was established. The Continental Albinos and Lutinos were of two different breeding kinds, the sex-linked and the non-linked, and there was no difference in their external colouring. In the early days of their importation to Britain these two kinds were mixed and gave the breeders many shocks by the unexpected results they produced!

10. A CHANGE OF FEATHER PATTERN

During 1933 there appeared spontaneously in Britain, Australia and Holland a new variety with a different arrangement of wing and mantle markings. In Britain the first birds were called marbled Budgerigars on account of their marbled colour effect. Later however, the Australian name of Opaline was universally adopted as being a more suitable title for the variety. All the separate mutations were practically identical in colouring and all sex-linked in their breeding behaviour. The Australian form was bred from a wild-caught Opaline Light Green hen and the British form from an Opaline Cobalt mutation, also a hen. About the same time as the Opalines appeared another sex-linked mutation was bred in Britain and was called the 'Slate'. The Slates were quickly produced in many shades but on account of their somewhat dull colour were not very popular with breeders, however they are now coming back in favour again.

11. MUTATION IN THEIR NATIVE COUNTRY

The year 1934 was quite an eventful one for the Budgerigar

Fancy. From their native country there came the beautifully, richly coloured Yellow-wings and White-wings with their vivid breast colour and almost clear wings. From Australia also, came another new breeding type and colour, the Australian Dominant Grey. Needless to say both these new varieties caused much discussion amongst Budgerigar breeders all over the world. In the same year another Grey mutant appeared in Britain, but unlike the Australian Grey this British type was Recessive in its manner of inheritance, although its colouring was practically the same. The British Grey has now gone out of existence.

12. A STARTLING MUTATION

In the year following the one that gave Clearwings and Greys, came a most startling new Dominant form, the Yellow-faced Blue group. These birds were reported from several places at the same time, each mutation being somewhat like the other and reproducing in nearly the same manner. These new birds dispelled the old idea that it was not possible to have yellow and white colouring on the same bird. Needless to say, the Yellow-faced birds caused a great deal of discussion and many arguments took place as to their hereditary character.

13. VARIEGATION OCCURS IN DENMARK

Since the early 1930s various odd specimens of Pied or Variegated birds have been bred, but the types were not fixed or even reproduced. About 1935 a true breeding race of yellow and green, and blue and white, Pied birds were raised in Denmark. Living specimens of this variety were not seen in Britain until 1948 where two Yellow and Green Pied birds were imported by the author from Finland where the original strain was being bred by one of the original breeders, Herr C. af Enehjelm.

14. FURTHER VARIEGATED FORMS APPEAR IN BELGIUM

It was during the 1939–45 war period that a further mutation of a variegated pattern appeared in Belgium where it was established. A few of these birds were imported into this country where a number of strains of various colours have been bred. Good specimens of this variety should look like normals except all primary flight feathers, long tail feathers and a patch at nape of neck are yellow or white according to which series they belong. These birds are usually known as White-flights and Yellow-flights.

15. INNUMERABLE COLOURS CAN BE PRODUCED

It is at once obvious to the breeder that by crossing the numerous colours and varieties together a very large range of fascinatingly coloured birds can be raised. Quite a lot of the more rare, and shall we say complicated colours, have yet to be bred as at present their being is only on paper. Since this book was first published in 1952 the Author has been successful in establishing a further new red-eyed variety. These birds are known as Lace-wing Whites and Lace-wing Yellows and are similar to normal Albinos and Lutinos except they have markings on head, neck, wings and tail of a lovely soft cinnamon shade. This attractive variety is sex-linked in its manner of inheritance and expectations can be calculated as for the other established sex-linked varieties. (See para. 104.)

CHAPTER 2

HOUSING

16. SELECTING ACCOMMODATION

ONE of the charms of breeding Budgerigars is that they can be housed under very varied conditions, in fact it is often said that they can be kept practically anywhere. It will be realised at once that there is a wide difference in just keeping birds and keeping them successfully in perfect health. In this chapter the housing of Budgerigars had been separated into three sections—cages, pens and aviaries, and each type will be dealt with in turn.

17. CAGES

At the present time the keeping and breeding of Budgerigars in cages is practised most extensively by Fanciers all over the world. Breeding in cages has quite a number of advantages over other methods especially in these days of limitations both of space and materials. Single pairs can be housed in a cage and the breeder is quite certain of the exact pedigree of all the young produced. It is an extremely important factor to know and have recorded the pedigrees of all stock and especially so when breeding for colour.

18. SIZE OF BREEDING AND STOCK CAGES

If the breeder is going to use cages it is as well to have them constructed to a uniform pattern; the exact size of course will be governed primarily by the amount of bird-room space available. However, it is important to make all the cages as large as possible to get the maximum amount of flight room. Cages should not be less in size than 36-in. long, 12-in. deep and 18-in. high, these measurements can be adjusted to suit individual conditions. If 15-in. is allowed for the wire part of the front it will leave some 3-in. for the bottom rail and sand tray and will help to prevent seed, etc. from being scattered about too freely (See

Fig. 1 for design). This type of cage can be converted into a stock cage by removing the nesting box and adjusting the perches.

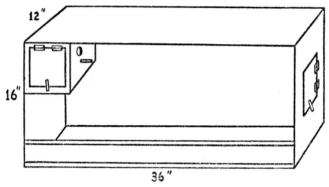

FIGURE 1.   BREEDING CAGE.

19. NESTING BOXES INSIDE CAGES

Quite an appreciable amount of space can be saved if nest boxes are put inside the cages instead of being fixed to the outside. With inside nest boxes, it is advisable to arrange them so that the inspection door can be opened from the outside to prevent undue disturbance of the nesting birds. Nest boxes can be of various patterns, but it is preferable not to have them less than 9-in. x 5-in. x 8-in. (See Fig. 2), all bottoms should be removable and the concave not less than $\frac{3}{4}$-in. deep in centre.

20. DECORATION

Cages can be painted both inside and outside with a good brand of non-poisonous enamel which is free from a lead base. Such paints can be obtained from all good Seed and Accessory Stores. Fine quality distemper or plastic emulsion paint can also be used for cage decoration and is much less in price than the paint and can of course be renewed each year if necessary, keeping the cages always fresh. Certain disinfectants and insecticides can be added when mixing distemper and will help to minimize the risk of that pest, the red mite.

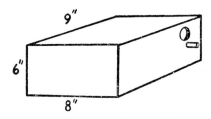

FIGURE 2A.   NEST BOX.

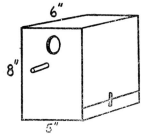

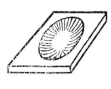

FIGURE 2B.   NEST BOX.

21. STANDARD SEED FOR CAGED BUDGERIGARS

When Budgerigars are housed in cages it will be realized that their restricted flight room will make it necessary for their diet to be of a less fattening nature than those in aviaries. Breeders have found after many years of experimenting that three parts small canary seed, one part white millet and one part Indian millet makes a good standard feed. When young are in the nest boxes a few whole oats or groats can be added to the mixture.

22. SEED AND WATER VESSELS

Vessels for seed, water and grit for use in cages are very varied in design and quite a number of materials such as glass, glazed pottery, metal and plastics are used in their construction. Fig. 3 gives some of the designs that are in general use and can be obtained from Seed and Accessory Stores. In addition to their usual seed Budgerigars require grit, cuttlefish bone, mineral

FIGURE 3.

blocks and green food: these items will be dealt with fully in a later chapter.

23. PERCHES

It is rather important that the perches in cages should be of varing thicknesses so that the birds' feet can get rest and exercise, thereby preventing stiffness. The practice of varying the sizes of perches should always be used in cages irrespective of the kind of birds they house. Care should be taken to see that all perches are made from non-poisonous wood as Budgerigars take a great delight in gnawing them and especially hens when breeding time draws near. Wood from all fruit trees is safe as are Hazel, Hawthorn, Alder, Sloe, Birch and Deal. The perches should be arranged so that they are not underneath one another, to prevent fouling by the birds' droppings.

24. PENS

Pens are small-sized aviaries without flights and are of very great value for breeding Budgerigars under control and at the same time allowing the birds a reasonable amount of freedom. The size of the pens, and the design of the bird room in which they are built, are naturally controlled by the amount of space at the breeder's disposal. A most useful size is 2-ft. 6-in. wide, 4-ft. deep and 6-ft–7-ft. high (see Fig 4) for a suggested layout for six or more pens. It is advisable to put only one pair per pen and breed under strict control, but should two pairs be used they should be both of the same colour. The management throughout is the same as with cage breeding.

25. AVIARIES

All other types of buildings used for breeding and keeping

Budgerigars are called aviaries and vary considerably in size and design. Many different materials can be used in their construc-

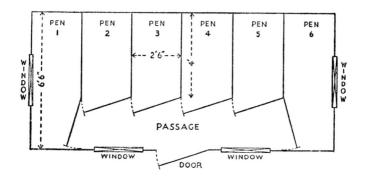

FIGURE 4. CONTROL PENS.

tion and buildings which have been used for other purposes are often converted into good aviaries with only a minimum amount of alteration. Plate III gives a design for a set of controlled flighted aviaries. These controlled aviaries are most useful for the breeder who has a reasonable amount of space and wishes to go in for breeding really seriously.

26. GARDEN ATTRACTION

If the breeder keeps a few pairs of Budgerigars solely for decoration and the amusement of the family there is no need for control and an aviary of the design as Plate IV will be found very suitable. In an aviary of this all sorts of little gadgets such as ladders, swing perches, swinging hoops, etc., can be fixed up for the birds' and also their owner's amusement. Decorative aviaries with varying coloured Budgerigars can make a garden very attractive and if a fish pond is included nearby a corner can become very beautiful. If the birds are not required for breeding, cock birds only are the best to keep.

27. THE DANGERS OF VERMIN

It is very important when building aviaries or bird-rooms to make them vermin proof as dreadful havoc can be wrought amongst the birds by night invaders. There are many ways in which aviaries or birdrooms can be protected, one method is to raise the floor of the sleeping quarters 12-in.–18-in. above ground level to allow dogs and cats free access. Although this is a good method it is not always practicable, whereas a concrete floor can be laid down anywhere, and used together with small mesh wire netting, will make the sleeping quarters quite safe. If the aviary is made of wood and standing on a concrete base, an 18-in. band of small mesh wire should be fixed all the way round the bottom, including the entrance door. A strip of sheet metal about 12-in. x 18-in. can be bent and fixed round each corner just above the wire and will stop rats from climbing up the corners and making an entrance under the eaves. A periodical inspection of the aviary or birdroom should be made to see if it is still vermin proof.

28. FLOOR COVERING

It is rather necessary to sprinkle fine gravel, sand or sawdust over cement or wooden floors to absorb surplus moisture and make cleaning easier. During the winter months sawdust will be found to be the best to use on a cement floor, it helps to minimize the cold from striking upwards.

29. DECORATING THE AVIARIES

The insides of all sleeping quarters should be given a coat of lime wash, a good distemper or plastic emulsion paint each year and the outsides either painted (non-poisonous paint) or treated with creosote or similar wood preservative. To lengthen the life of outside wire netting it can be given a coat of non-poisonous paint when first fixed and this should be allowed to get perfectly dry before putting the birds into the aviary. Untreated wire netting must be thoroughly brushed with a stiff brush, to remove loose particles of galvanizing which are extremely dangerous and often cause death to birds when put in new quarters.

CHAPTER 3

STOCK

30. BUYING STOCK

FOLLOWING the completion of the bird room or aviary, the next step is to acquire some birds, which can be obtained either from a local breeder or bird shop or from answering an advertisement in the Fancy Press. When the birds are bought locally or from away they should be had on approval and examined thoroughly before making a definite purchase. If this is done the new Fancier will have no reason to complain as having bought something unknown and satisfaction will be achieved on both sides. It will take the breeder a number of years to build up an exhibition strain and it will be realized that this is something that cannot be hurried. With Budgerigars as with all livestock it takes a considerable amount of patience and foresight to form a strain.

31. BEST TIME TO BUY

It is really a matter of opinion whether it is best to buy fully adult birds ready for breeding at the beginning of the season or to get young ones later in the year in readiness for the following season's breeding operations. If young birds are bought, their price is invariably less than adults, also they will have plenty of time to settle down in their new quarters and will often breed more freely. The young birds should be early hatched, if possible, so that they can be used for breeding the next year. There is one snag in buying unmoulted young birds, particularly with certain colours, and that is it is not possible to tell their correct colour and they are often difficult to sex. Later in another chapter the colours of birds will be dealt with very fully.

32. BEST COLOURS FOR THE NEW BREEDER

Once the breeder has decided where and when to get the birds

19

the next thing to do is to decide what colour or colours are to be kept. Visiting an established breeder's aviary, or a bird shop, for the first time, the beginner is dazzled by the sight of so many different colours and varieties that it is hard to decide what birds to have. Should this be the case then the best thing to do is to take the advice of the breeder. All the different colours and varieties breed equally well, and only difference being with individual pairs of birds.

33. CHANGE OF SHADE

The peculiarity with certain varieties of a distinct difference of colouring between adult and young birds, may be at first quite puzzling and often leads the new breeder to think the same birds are different colours. Take for instance young Cobalts, who in the nest feather, are a soft violet tinted powder blue, whereas their adult plumage is a hard, bright, deep cobalt shade. Again with young Mauves, they look quite grey in their nest feather, but when adult, assume that definite deep mauve colour. When buying young unmoulted birds of certain varieties for show there is always a risk that they will not moult out quite the desired exhibition shade of colour. All show birds should be bought when they have their full plumage and their markings and colour can be judged.

34. BIRDS TRAVELLING FROM A DISTANCE

It is advisable when buying new birds from any distance where the climate conditions may be different, to find out just how they have been housed. When birds are bought from say a closed bird room on the south-eastern side of England, it is hardly fair to put them straight out into an open flight aviary in Scotland. Although Budgerigars are one of the hardiest of birds, they do need a little special care and attention when they are changing quarters. (See Fig. 5.)

35. POINTS TO NOTE

When new stock is required only fully feathered healthy birds should be bought from a reliable breeder or shop, making certain that the birds' beaks, feet and legs are not malformed and that there are no growths on the body. The fact that birds may have a missing toenail or so, does not matter in the least with

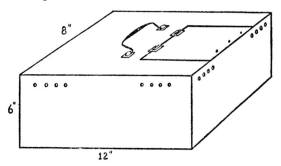

FIGURE 5. TRAVEL BOX.

stock birds, but it is extremely important with exhibition birds. Birds wearing closed, year dated rings, should always be bought as this will be a guarantee as to the age of the stock. Old or over fat birds are of little use in breeding quarters and should be avoided even if they do seem to have that little extra size. The purchase of closed ringed stock cannot be too fully stressed as many birds not wearing closed rings are being imported from Europe and it is therefore impossible to tell their age. Young birds can be bought in their unmoulted state whether they are ringed or not but of course it is always a gamble to know how these 'bar-headed' birds will moult for colour and markings.

CHAPTER 4

FEEDING

36. BIRDS OF SIMPLE TASTES

ONE of the many joys of keeping Budgerigars is the fact that they are so very easy to feed and do not require masses of soft, messy foods. During the non-breeding season a good standard mixture for birds housed in aviaries, is half small canary seed and half yellow and white millet with a few whole clipped oats or groats added occasionally. When the young are in the nest, then a mixture of two parts small canary, one part large canary, one part white millet and an extra quantity of whole oats or groats should be used. It is best to buy loose seeds in bulk and blend the mixtures as required. Red millet should be avoided as it contains little real food value although it is sometimes used in mixed packet seeds. The small yellow Indian millet either in sprays or loose is most useful, particularly in encouraging young birds to eat and to tempt adult birds when training for show work.

37. SPECIAL FEEDING WHEN BREEDING

During the breeding season when the young have hatched, it has been found beneficial both to the parents and youngsters to offer the birds periodically a little of one of the patent canary soft foods or an insectivorous mixture made crumbly moist. This is not absolutely necessary, but Budgerigars in their wild state are like many other seed eating birds and eat any insects they find when feeding, in the seeding grasses which form their staple diet. The use of soft food must not be too free, otherwise the would-be benefits are cancelled by the birds digestive organs being upset.

38. GREEN FOODS

Without a doubt, good clean green food plays a tremendous part in the rearing of strong healthy Budgerigar chicks. There are many kinds of green foods which the birds eat with relish, the foremost being chickweed, seeding grasses and spinach. During the off seasons for the green foods mentioned above, young dandelion leaves, lettuce (small quantities only), heart of cabbage, carrot, apple, etc., can be used. Great care must always be taken to see that any green food is quite fresh and has not been fouled by animals or chemical manures or sprays. Should there be the least doubt as to its cleanliness, the green should be well washed and dried before it is given to the birds. During the winter months, frosted green foods must be avoided as these are very dangerous and will cause stomach trouble, often with fatal results. If the birds have not been used to green food it should be given to them only in small quantities at first. Do not give the birds too much at a time so that it is left about in the cage, pen or aviary to get stale or fouled. Another important item to the birds' diet particularly at breeding time is grit: a regular supply must *always* be available. Good grits for Budgerigars can be obtained from bird shops and seed stores. Clean sand or grit from the sea shore are very good and contain certain minerals which are beneficial to health and growth. Likewise from the sea shore comes cuttlefish bone, the great source of lime for all caged birds, this also can be bought from seed and bird shops. Soaked, sprouted seeds (oats, wheat, etc.) can be used as green food during the periods when ordinary green food is in short supply or not in season. The cereal should be placed in flat shallow earthenware pans, soaked in cold water and put in a warm dark place until the shoots are about half an inch long. This sprouted seed should be given only in small quantities at first but it can be used at any time during the year.

39. SEED HOPPERS

There is a very wide range of seed hoppers—some large, some small, on the market, all of which serve the purpose of providing the birds with sufficient quantity of seed for several days. Hoppers are of special value in aviaries when the owner has to leave the birds to their own devices for days at a time. Care should be taken to see that the hoppers are always full of *seed* and not husk and seed, at the beginning of each period. Many birds have died through their owners not realising that the hoppers have been full of husks and not seed.

40. WATER

It is very important for Budgerigars to always have a supply of fresh clean water. During the non-breeding seasons the birds do not drink very much, however when growing chicks are in the nest boxes quite a considerable amount is consumed. Although Budgerigars do not bathe freely like many other kinds of birds they often get great enjoyment splashing about in their water pots, for this reason it is preferable to use flat shallow glazed pots. A few drops of tincture of iodine in the water once a week is beneficial to the birds, the quantity used is three to four drops of iodine to a wineglass of water. It is mentioned above that Budgerigars do not bathe much but what they like is to roll in wet grass. For this purpose sods of clean grass well watered, should be put into the pens or aviaries at frequent periods particularly during the summer months. Much amusement can be obtained by watching the birds playing about in the wet grass.

CHAPTER 5

BREEDING

41. CONDITION FOR BREEDING

IT is most essential that birds are in perfect breeding condition before they are allowed to attempt to breed. If the birds are not in condition then weakly chicks, infertile eggs or no eggs at all, will invariably result. Breeding condition and show condition have two different meanings; with the latter not only have the birds to be fit but also all their feathers must be perfect whereas with breeding condition the state of the feathers is only a secondary condition; the birds themselves must be in tiptop condition; When cock birds are in full breeding condition the cere (the smooth patch just above the upper part of the beak) is a bright shining blue in all colours except the red-eyed and Recessive pied birds where it takes a soft purplish tone. With hen birds the cere in full condition is quite different being a deep chocolate and quite rough. Should the cere of any adult hens suddenly turn a pale washy blue, it is a sign that they are going out of condition and need closely watching to see that they are not really sick. The same thing applies to adult cock birds, only the cere here does not become so pale as with out-of-condition hens.

42. BEST TIME TO START BREEDING

The newcomer to the Fancy would be well advised not to be in too much of a hurry to start breeding operations. The end of February or the beginning of March is quite time enough to pair up the birds as by then the hours of daylight are longer and there is very little chance of long spells of cold weather. When breeding is commenced too soon any chicks hatched are deprived of getting regular supplies of fresh green food which is very important in rearing healthy vigorous youngsters. The breeders who wish to show moulted young stock at early Autumn shows will often start breeding rather sooner than they would otherwise.

However, the beginner is wise not to try this until Budgerigars have been bred for a few seasons and experience in their many habits has been gained. Over keenness to start so often results in disappointments by the most choice birds getting into difficulties which may prove fatal.

43. SELECTING THE INITIAL STOCK

Undoubtedly the right choice of the original breeding stock is most important as new breeders can so easily be disillusioned by making a bad start. Birds should not be bought without careful forethought and then always bought on approval. It cannot be emphasised too strongly that only birds with closed, year-dated rings, should be considered when forming the original stud. Unringed stock have no guarantee as to age or breeding and the knowledge of the stock's pedigree is so very necessary as it will be disclosed in later chapters.

44. NESTING RECEPTACLES

Wooden nesting boxes with removable concave bottoms are without a shadow of doubt the best type for Budgerigars, the old type of nests, the cocoanut husks, have for obvious reasons gone right out of use in this country. Figs. 2a and 2b are two designs of nesting boxes which can be bought from Bird Accessory Stores or they can be made by the breeder. The best design to use is really a matter of individual taste providing they have a deep removable concave base and an inspection door. Wooden nest boxes are so easy to keep clean and free from mite pests and can be scalded and re-creosoted or emulsion painted after use each season and with care will last for many years. The birds should be allowed to thoroughly settle down in their breeding quarters before the nest boxes are introduced. Nest boxes should be hung facing the light and if more than one pair are breeding together they should all be hung at the same level, allowing two boxes to each pair. To prevent eggs from getting dented or smashed, the boxes must be firmly fixed to the side of the aviary to prevent wobble. A little coarse pine sawdust can be put into the concave of each box to prevent the eggs from rolling about too freely on the bare wood and to absorb excess moisture.

45. WATCH FOR FIGHTING

When there are several pairs of Budgerigars breeding together in one enclosure a certain amount of squabbling invariably takes place when the nest boxes are first hung. A little good humoured fighting for the boxes does not do any harm but a watch should be kept to see that real serious and vicious fighting is not taking place. Occasionally two hens will want the same box although there are plenty of others to choose from and each bird sets about the other with the object to maim or kill. The best way to overcome this and to prevent a casualty is to remove the disputed box. When this is done the hens usually settle down and choose other boxes without further trouble.

46. PERIOD OF INCUBATION

Budgerigars lay clutches of eggs varying in number from three to ten with five or six being the most usual number. Eggs are laid on alternate days, the incubation period of seventeen or eighteen days starts from the laying of the first egg, so in a clutch of five eggs the eldest chick is ten days old before the last has hatched. Budgerigars are mostly very good mothers and care for the youngest chick with equal attention as they do their first born. The nest boxes can be inspected occasionally whilst the birds are still incubating to see if things are going smoothy on their natural course. During dry weather it is a good thing to damp the eggs with a little warm water a day or two before they are due to hatch. If the eggs get too dry and the inner skin hard, the chicks may not be able to break out and will die in the shell, but damping helps to prevent this from happening. When the young hatch it is necessary to look into the boxes more frequently to ring the young, remove any bad eggs or dead chicks and renew sawdust to keep the boxes sweet and clean. Young Budgerigars leave their nests when they are fully fledged at about five or six weeks old. The young should be left with their parents for about six or seven days after the *last* chick has flown; by this time they should all be able to feed on their own. It is advisable to remove them so that the adults are not hampered in preparing for their second brood. Quite often the hens will start laying their next clutch of eggs before the last chick has left the box. The youngsters should be removed to their new quarters early in the day so that they have the maximum amount of daylight to find their bearings and settle down before dusk. Youngsters are best housed entirely on their own until they have assumed their adult plumage.

47. SEXING YOUNGSTERS

If the breeder has sufficient space it is by far the best to keep the sexes apart as soon as they are removed from the breeding aviaries. The sexing of young birds is best carried out when they are about six weeks old as at this time the margin of error is likely to be small. With the young cocks, the cere is more prominent, rounder and deeper in colour than it is in the young hens and although this is not a guarantee of correctness it mostly proves to be right.

48. IDENTIFICATION OF BIRDS

There is no surer way of identifying any birds than the closed ring method: these rings are put on when the chicks are between five and eight days old and stay on for life. As the size of the feet of individual nests of young vary, it is necessary to watch the chicks from about five days old so that their feet do not become too big for the rings to pass over. Rings can be put on as follows: the chick should be held in one hand with one foot held between the thumb and first finger then the ring should be slipped over the two longest toes, along over the foot and up the leg pulling the two remaining toes through the ring with a small pointed stick (a matchstick is a good implement for this purpose). Although the young may squeak quite a lot whilst ringing is in progress it does not really hurt them and they settle down at once when put back in their nest box. Rings can be bought from Messrs. Hughes, High Street, Hampton Hill, Middlesex, the well-known makers of all kinds of bird and poultry rings. One type of ring is coloured metal with a different colour for each year and they can also bear the year date, number and code or initials of the breeder. These coloured metal rings are most useful for telling the year of a bird's birth without actually having to catch it up and examine the ring.

LAYOUT FOR A BREEDING REGISTER

Colour　　　　　　　　　　　　　　　Sex　　　　　Hatched

Breeder
Ring No.

	Nest Feather	Adult Feather
Mask		
Body		
Vent and Thighs		
Rump		
Claws		
Legs		
Tail		
Wings		

Sire				Dam			
Ring No.				Ring No.			
Grand Sire		Grand Dam		Grand Sire		Grand Dam	
G.G.S.	G.G.D.	G.G.S.	G.G.D.	G.G.S.	G.G.D.	G.G.S.	G.G.D.

NOTES:—

49. JOIN A SOCIETY

All breeders are advised to join a Budgerigar Club or Society of which there are many both local and ones dealing with areas and special colours; also there is the Budgerigar Society with membership for the whole world. Since its commencement in 1925 the Budgerigar Society has and still is doing good work for the advancement of the Budgerigar Fancy as a whole. In addition to literature and special show prizes the members of the Budgerigar Society are given a special code number to put on their own rings so that birds wearing them can always be traced back to their original breeders.

50. STOCK RECORDING

It is of the utmost importance that an accurate breeding register is kept and maintained and an example of a general layout will be found on page 29. In addition to such things as date of pairing, colour and ring numbers of parents and young, date of first egg and chick, little items such as any dead in shell, peculiar behaviour of either cock or hen should be written down. In fact the register should be a complete record of the history of all the stock. When the breeder is specially interested in the production of new and rare colours, the breeding register will be invaluable in tracing why unexpected colours have turned up in the nests. Show successes can also be recorded and it is of much interest and help to trace these successes through the various families.

CHAPTER 6

COLOUR DESCRIPTIONS

51. EXPLANATION OF COLOURS

IN the following paragraphs a brief description will be given of all the well-known colours in addition to quite a number of the lesser known ones. It is not possible in a small handbook to give a full account of every colour and shade, but those given will enable the breeder to envisage many rare and beautiful types which would otherwise only be names.

52. GREENS

Light Green is the original colour of the Budgerigar and from them all other shades have been evolved during the last hundred years. The chest, underparts, thighs and rump are bright light grass green: the mask is bright yellow and the lower part is ornamented by six evenly placed round black spots forming a necklace at each end of which is a small bright violet cheek patch covering the last spot each side. The back of head, nape of neck, shoulders and wings are black, grey and yellow marked in undulated lines; these markings have given rise to one of the many names, Zebra Parrakeet, by which the Budgerigar was originally known. The eyes are very dark brown, the beak horn coloured and the feet and legs can be either dull blue or pink. DARK GREENS: these are the same as Light Greens except that the body colour is a deep rich dark green shade. OLIVE GREENS: the markings are similar to those of the other Greens with the body shade being a deep bronze olive green colouring, sometimes flecked on rump and thigh with dark green feathers. The yellow ground colour in Olive Greens is decidedly deeper in tone than in the other two green forms.

53. YELLOWS

With the Light Yellow birds there is a very great difference in

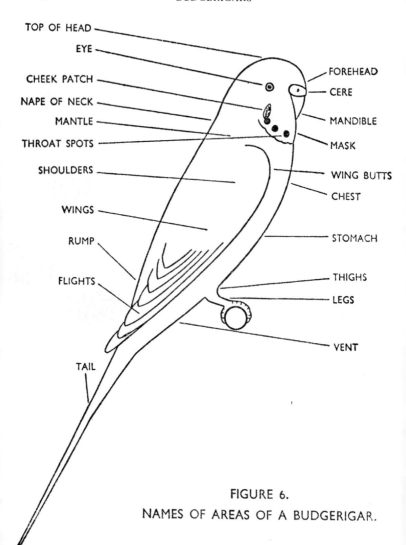

FIGURE 6.
NAMES OF AREAS OF A BUDGERIGAR.

PLATE I. Champion Sky Blue Cock, many times best
Budgerigar in Show.

Photo: T. C. Charlton.

PLATE II.

Champion Light Green Cock

Photo: R. D. Knight

PLATE III. (*above*) Outdoor flighted aviary of good design.

PLATE IV.
(*below*) A well furnished Birdroom with breeding cages and resting flights.

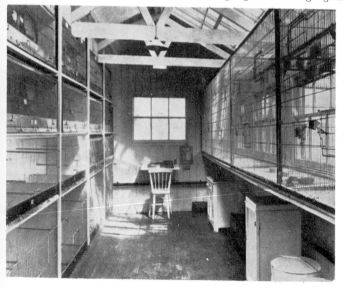

the purity of their colouring, so much so that the newcomer could quite easily take the two extremes as being different varieties. The exhibition type of Light Yellows, sometimes called Buttercup Yellows, are a clear rich yellow throughout, with only the very faintest ghostlike markings on their wings and a bluish flush on their long tail feathers. With exhibition Light Yellows the characteristic throat spots are absent and the cheek patches assume a silvery shade. The beak is horn colour, the eyes dark and the feet and legs can be either pink or dull blue. DARK YELLOWS: these are the same as the Light Yellows only the colour is much deeper throughout. A very few really clear Dark Yellows exist, the majority have a decided dark green tinting, specially on their rumps. OLIVE YELLOWS: these are similar to the Dark Yellows only the body shade is a golden green tint and a few specimens have been bred where the colour is almost a clear orange.

54. GREYWING GREENS

The Light Green form of the Greywing Green has a body colour the shade of young beech leaves and the markings, including the throat spots, are of a brownish grey tone. The tail is a deep dull blue and the legs and feet dull blue or pink, the beak is horn coloured and the eyes dark. Perhaps the best way to describe the colouring of Greywings is to say they are midway between that of green and yellow. However, Greywings are a separate mutation and not produced by the simple method of crossing together of ordinary green and yellow birds. GREYWING DARK GREENS: these birds are the same as the Greywing Light Greens except that the body colour is a rich bright pale dark green. GREYWING OLIVE GREENS: the markings of these birds are the same as the Greywing Light and Dark Greens but the yellow ground colour is a much richer tone. The whole body colour is a beautiful dull golden shade which is set off to advantages by the dark brownish grey of the wing markings and throat spots.

55. CINNAMON GREENS

In the Cinnamon Light Greens the chest, underparts, thighs and rump are a particularly attractive shade of soft pale light green. The mask is clear yellow and the lower part is ornamented with six evenly placed spots of a cinnamon brown colour: the cheek patches are bright light violet. The back of head, nape of neck, shoulders and wings are marked with undulations of pure cinnamon brown and quite free from any blackness. The markings where carried by Cinnamon cock birds are invariably a little darker in shade than those of the hens and this applies to all the different Cinnamon varieties. CINNAMON DARK GREENS: these birds are the same as the Cinnamon Light Green except that the body colour is a soft dark green shade, solid and even throughout. CINNAMON OLIVE GREENS: these birds are the same as the Cinnamon Light and Dark Greens except that the body colour is a very beautiful golden olive shade and the markings throughout are a shade richer in tone.

56. CINNAMON YELLOWS

The Cinnamon Light Yellows are very similar to the ordinary Light Yellows and it is often very difficult for breeders to tell one from the other. As a general rule the Cinnamon Light Yellows are very clear in colour throughout and any markings that may show on the wing butts are very pale indeed. The yellow colouring carried by these birds is very pure and rich in tone and the birds themselves have a soft warm look about their feathers. The feet are always pink and the beak is a bright horn colour and the cheek patches take on a soft silvery appearance. CINNAMON DARK YELLOWS: these birds are the same as the Cinnamon Light Yellows except that the yellow colour is of a decidedly deeper tone. The Cinnamon Dark Yellows are much easier to distinguish from the ordinary Dark Yellows by the fact that their colour is so much more free from any green tinting. CINNAMON OLIVE YELLOWS: these birds are of a very rich golden shade and the good clear specimens are very beautiful indeed. The purity of the colour in all the Cinnamon Yellow types depends on the colour of the stock from which they are produced.

57. OPALINE GREENS

The Opaline Light Greens are very handsome birds, the head and part the way down the neck is rich yellow faintly ticked with dark markings. The mantle (shoulders) is bright green and the wings are heavily suffused with bright rich green. On the primary flights is a light patch which is quite clear and distinct. The general chest, flanks, underparts and rump are an intense bright light green of a shade found only in the Opalines. The tail is mainly light greenish blue surrounded by a dark blue edging. These characteristic markings on mantle, wings and tail are carried by all the different Opaline forms. OPALINE DARK GREENS: these are the same as the Opaline Light Greens except the body; mantle and suffusion are of a brilliant shade of dark green. The Opaline Dark Greens are very lovely birds and are perhaps the most brilliantly coloured of all the green series of Budgerigars. OPALINE OLIVE GREENS: these are the same as the Opaline Light and Dark Greens except that the body, mantle and wing suffusion are of a very attractive shade of rich olive green.

58. YELLOW-WING GREENS (CLEARWING GREENS)

In the Yellow-wing Light Greens the chest, underparts, thighs and rump are a clear light green colour ranging from 75% to 90% of the depth of shade carried by normal Light Greens. The head, nape of neck, shoulders and wings are almost a clear yellow and it is this contrast between wings and body colour that gives these birds such a handsome appearance. The clearness of the yellow areas varies with individual birds, the ideal being quite clear yellow. YELLOW-WING DARK GREENS: these are the same as the Yellow-wing Light Greens except that the body shade is a very deep rich dark green, quite a distinct and beautiful shade. The contrast between the wings and body colour is shown up to the greatest advantage in these birds. YELLOW-WING OLIVE GREENS: these are the same as the Yellow-wing Light and Dark Greens except that the body colour is deep olive green more golden in shade than the colour of normal Olive Greens.

59. FALLOW GREENS

Although these birds are called Greens, and they are genetically, their body shade actually tends much more towards yellow than it does green. All Fallows vary quite a lot in the shade of their body colouring. The chest is generally a soft greenish tinted yellow and the colour becomes more green on the underpart, thighs and rump. The markings on nape of neck, shoulders, wings and throat spots are a dark brown similar to the colour which is carried by the Cinnamon varieties. The feet and legs are pink, the beak orange and the eyes are quite distinct from the normal varieties, being a deep rich red. FALLOW DARK GREENS: these are the same as the Fallow Light Greens except that the body colour is much more of a golden yellow olive shade than it is dark green. In fact Fallow Dark Greens are frequently confused with Fallow Olives. FALLOW OLIVE GREENS: these birds are the same as the Fallow Light and Dark Greens except that their body colour is a lovely deep shade of golden yellow with the rump being rich yellow olive.

60. FALLOW YELLOWS

The ideal Fallow Light Yellows should be a clear bright yellow throughout with deep red eyes, orange beak and pink feet and legs. However, the majority of Fallow Light Yellows show faint brown markings on nape of neck, shoulders and wings and the long tail feathers have a ver pale violet blue tinting. Good clear Fallow Yellows can easily be mistaken for Lutinos unless the breeder had had considerable experience with both types. There are also two other lightly marked Fallows—the Fallow Greywing Light Green and the Fallow Yellow-wing Light Green. FALLOW DARK YELLOWS: these are the same as the Fallow Light Yellows, only the yellow colouring throughout is quite a deeper shade. There are also Fallow Greywing Dark Greens and Fallow Yellow-wing Dark Greens. FALLOW OLIVE YELLOWS: these are the same as the Fallow Light and Dark Greens, only the yellow colouring throughout is a rich golden orange shade and is one of the most attractive colours. There are also Fallow Greywing Olive Greens and Fallow Yellow-wing Olive Greens.

61. LUTINOS (CLEAR YELLOW RED-EYES)

These birds are generally known in the Fancy as Lutinos and are clear yellow all through without even the ghost-like markings as often seen in Fallow Yellows. The beak is bright orange and the eyes are deep red with light iris ring, the feet and legs bright pink.

62. GREY GREENS

With the Grey Light Greens the chest, underparts, flanks and rump, are an even clear light olive quite free from any ordinary green tinting. The markings on nape of neck, shoulders and wings are clear cut black on yellow and the long tail feathers are dull black. The cheek patches are light silvery grey and quite distinct from those carried by normally coloured birds. These birds are also called Dominant Greys and Australian Greys but they are all one and the same. There is however a Recessive Grey variety but the colouring is practically identical. GREY DARK GREENS AND GREY OLIVE GREENS: these birds are the same as the Grey Light Greens, only their body colours are of correspondingly darker shades. There are also Grey Green forms of Opaline Greens, Greywing Greens, Cinnamon Greens, Yellows, Yellowwings, Fallow Greens and Pied Greens in all the three shades of each variety.

63. VIOLET GREENS

It seems rather strange to call birds Violet Greens when they are an actual green colour and do not show violet in their plumage. These birds are called by that name for the want of a more suitable one because the violet factor which causes their strange green colouring is a Dominant one, the same as the Grey factor. By adding the Violet factor to Light Green it causes the birds to assume a pale dark green colour of a most unusual tone and added to the dark green it makes them take on an exceedingly dark metallic dark green shade. It also deepens very considerably the colour of the Olive Green birds. There can be a Violet Green kind of all the other existing green forms including Yellow, Cinnamon, Pied and Fallow types.

64. RECESSIVE PIED GREENS

These birds are also called Variegateds, Bi-colours and on the Continent, Harlequins, and as these various names indicate they have a most unusual arrangement of their colouring. With all the Pied Green kinds the largest areas of colour are a particularly clear lemon yellow. The nape of neck, shoulders, wings and tail are irregularly marked by ticks or patches of undulations in black, grey, cinnamon or ghost markings according to the type to which they belong. A large number of Pieds have the top part of their chest clear yellow with an irregular patch of vivid green on the lower part and the rump may be either clear or marked with the same green colour as the chest. The area of dark feathers varies with each bird, or group of birds, and some may be almost clear and others nearly all dark and all grades in between. It may be possible by careful selective breeding to produce quite clear birds (the same as Lutinos only with dark eyes), and also evenly marked birds. A dark eyed clear yellow form was first produced on the Continent and these birds are also being bred in England in Yellow, White and Yellow-faced White forms. The feet and legs are pink, the beak bright orange coloured and the eyes dark, solid reddish plum coloured, without the usual white iris ring. There can be a Pied form of all the other green and yellow types mentioned in the preceding paragraphs.

65. YELLOW FLIGHTED GREENS

These birds are somewhat similar in colour to some Pieds only they have quite an independent breeding behaviour. Ideal specimens should have a clear yellow spot at the nape of neck with clear yellow flights and tail, all the rest of the body and wings being dark according to the colour to which they belong. A number of birds do not come up to the ideal and quite a lot of skill is needed to produce birds with the correct markings: well marked birds are very handsome indeed.

66. YELLOW-FACED GREENS

These birds are really only a breeding type as it is practically impossible to distinguish with any degree of certainty between them and ordinary well-coloured Greens. There can be a Yellow-faced Green form of all existing Green types and the type which shows the Yellow-faced character to the best advantage in the Green form is the Yellow-faced Opaline Dark Green. Some of these Yellow-faced Green birds are a very beautiful colour indeed but are not of a sufficient difference to be readily recognized by Fanciers as a distinct type.

67. SLATE GREENS

These birds have a colouring which is about mid-way between that of the normal Green type and their Grey Green counterparts and consequently are not a very striking and outstanding range of colours. At the present time not many of these birds are in existence, but as they are a sex-linked form it is quite possible that odd specimens may turn up from unexpected sources from time to time. (The following chapter will show how this can come about.) There can be a Slate form of all the existing types of Greens and Yellows.

68. BLUES

Sky Blues are the Blue counterparts of the wild type Light Greens and were the first of the blue coloured series to appear as a mutation. The chest, underparts, thighs and rump are a clear even sky blue shade. The mask is clear white and the lower part is ornamented by six evenly placed, round black spots forming a necklace, at each end of which is a small violet cheek patch partly covering the last spot on each side. The nape of neck, shoulders and wings are black and grey on a white ground, some cock birds carry a little blue suffusion on nape of neck. The two central tail feathers are dark blue, the feet and legs blue or dull pink and the beak horn coloured. COBALTS: these birds which are sometimes known as Dark Blues or Powder Blues are the same as the Sky Blues except that the body colour is a lovely deep shade of cobalt. The cobalt shades are possibly the most popular colours with Budgerigar Fanciers generally. MAUVES: these birds are the same as the Sky Blues and Cobalts except that their body colour is a greyish mauve shade and is often flecked on flanks and rump with odd cobalt feathers. Originally these birds were known as Lilacs and Lavenders at that time (the late twenties) they were certainly more of a lilac colour than are the greyish hued Mauves as known to-day.

69. WHITES

With the White Sky Blues there is a big difference in the actual depth of the blue suffusion on the breast carried by individual birds, some are almost pure white and others have a very pronounced blue suffusion. The difference can be so great that the White birds are split into two sub types—the Whites of light suffusion and the Whites of deep suffusion and this applies to all the different White kinds. The chest, underparts, flanks and rump are a lightly or deeply suffused sky blue. With the exhibition Whites of light suffusion the characteristic throat spots are absent (it is immaterial with the deeply suffused birds) and the cheek patches vary in colour from a silvery tint to a pale violet. The nape of neck, shoulders and wings are faintly marked with bluish grey undulations. The beak is horn coloured, and eyes dark and the feet and legs dull pink or blue. WHITE COBALTS: these are the same as the White Blues except that the body colour is of a pale cobalt tint. White Cobalts are mostly of the deeply suffused kind and only very few lightly suffused birds exist. WHITE MAUVES: these are the same as the White Blues and White Cobalts except that the body colour is of a pale greyish mauve, but unlike the White Cobalts the suffusion is mostly light.

70. GREYWING BLUES

The Sky Blue form of the Greywing Green has a clear light blue shade on chest, underparts, flanks and rump, the ideal colour being mid-way between that of the normal Sky Blue and the White Sky Blue. The markings on nape of neck, shoulders and wings and the throat spots are pure grey and free from blackness. The long tail feathers are dull deep blue and the legs and feet are dull pink or blue with the beak horn coloured and the eyes dark. GREY-WING COBALTS: these are the same as the Greywing Blues except that the body colour is of a light bright cobalt. The Greywing Cobalts always seem to be the most popular colour of the Greywing group because of their soft pleasing shade. GREYWING MAUVES: these birds are the same as the Greywing Blues and Greywing Cobalts except that the body colour is a light greyish mauve. The body colour being the shade it is there is little contrast between it and the grey of the wing markings. Although not particularly attractive in colour Greywing Mauves are most useful in the breeding quarters for the production of the desired Greywing Cobalts.

71. CINNAMON BLUES

In the Cinnamon Blues the chest, underparts, flanks and rump are a lovely soft shade of pale blue. The mask is clear white, the lower part of which is ornamented with six evenly placed spots of a cinnamon brown colour and the cheek patches are of a light violet shade. The back of head, nape of neck, shoulders and wings are clearly marked with undulations of a definite pure cinnamon brown colour and quite free from any sign of blackness. The general appearance of all the Cinnamon group is of soft tightly feathered birds. CINNAMON COBALTS: these birds are the same as the Cinnamon Blues except that the body colour is a particularly nice shade of soft cobalt with a distinct violet gleam. CINNAMON MAUVES: these birds are the same as the Cinnamon Blues and Cinnamon Cobalts except that the body colour is a clear lavender mauve and is certainly one of the most attractive shades of colour in all the mauve birds.

72. CINNAMON WHITES

The Cinnamon White Blues are very much like the normal White Blue but the majority of them carry only the very faintest suffusion. Except for the fact that the cheek patches have a peculiar pale pinkish violet tone it is not possible to distinguish them clearly and quickly from ordinary white birds. The markings on nape of neck, shoulders and wings are exceedingly faint and of a light cinnamon tone and in some specimens the markings are non-existent except when viewed from certain angles. The feet and legs are pink, the beak a light horn colour and the eyes dark. CINNAMON WHITE COBALTS: these birds are the same as the Cinnamon White Blues except that the body colour is a light violet cobalt which varies in depth of shade with individual birds. CINNAMON WHITE MAUVES: these birds are the same as the Cinnamon White Blues and Cinnamon White Cobalts except that the body colour is of a very light shade of violet mauve and with some birds it has a definite pinkish tone.

73. OPALINE BLUES

The Opaline Blues are very beautifully coloured birds; the head and upper parts of the neck are a clear white lightly marked with dark grey tickings. The mantle (shoulders) is vivid blue and the wings are heavily suffused with the same brilliant colouring. On the primary flight feathers there is a white patch which is quite clear and distinct. The chest, underparts, flanks and rump are of an intense blue of a brightness seen only in the Opaline varieties. The tail is mainly white surrounded by a dark blue edging. The characteristic markings of the Opalines are carried by all the different types of Opalines irrespective of their colouring. OPALINE COBALTS: these are the same as the Opaline Blues except that the body, shoulders and suffusion are of a lovely bright shade of cobalt. Opaline Cobalts are very pleasing birds in appearance and have a particular attraction all of their own. OPALINE MAUVES: these are the same as the Opaline Blues and Opaline Cobalts except that the body, shoulders and suffusion are of a bright mauve shade generally with a few fleckings of cobalt on rump and flanks.

74. WHITE-WING BLUES (CLEARWING BLUES)

With the White-wing Blues the chest, underparts, flanks and rump are a clear blue colour ranging from 75% to 90% of the normal shade as carried by ordinary blue birds. The head, nape of neck, shoulders and wings are almost clear white making a fine contrast between wing and body colour. The clearness of the white areas varies with individual birds, the ideal being pure or paper white as it is often called. The beak is horn coloured the eyes dark and the feet and legs dull pink or blue. The actual blue colouring carried by the White-wing birds is a little brighter or harder in tone than the normal blue colouring. WHITE-WING COBALTS: these are the same as the White-wing Blues except that the body colour is a very rich shade of cobalt making the contrast between body and wings very sharp and clear. WHITE-WING MAUVES: these are the same as the White-wing Blues and White-wing Cobalts except that the body shade is of a dark bright mauve but it is often flecked on rump and flanks with cobalt feathers.

75. FALLOW BLUES

Although these birds are named Fallow Blues their body

Opaline sky blue Budgerigar

Green Budgerigar : cock

Opaline grey green Budgerigar

Blue Pied Budgerigar : cock

Lutino Budgerigar

Blue Budgerigar cock with three youngsters

Budgerigar cock : grey chesty!

Green Budgerigar

shade tends rather more towards white than it does blue. Fallow Blues vary quite a lot in the depth of their body colouring; this is controlled by the original stock by which they are produced. The chest is mostly a soft bluish tinted white and the colour becomes more blue as it nears the underparts, flanks and rump. The markings on nape of neck, shoulders and wings and the throat spots are a dark shade of brown. The feet and legs are pink and the beak bright orange with the eyes being a deep rich red. FALLOW COBALTS: these are the same as the Fallow Blues except that the body colour is a soft purplish cobalt shade which often makes it difficult to distinguish them from lightly coloured Fallow Mauves. FALLOW MAUVES: these are the same as the Fallow Blues and the Fallow Cobalts except that the body colour is of a warm violet mauve often heavily suffused on the flanks with cobalt feathers. It takes quite a time for the breeder to become proficient in identifying the two darker Fallows.

76. FALLOW WHITES

The ideal Fallow White Blues should be clear white throughout with deep red eyes, orange beaks and pink feet and legs. The majority of Fallow Whites show faint brown markings on nape of neck, shoulders and wings with the long tail feathers having a very pale violet blue tinting. There are also two other lightly marked Fallows—the Fallow Greywing Blues and the Fallow White-wing Blues. FALLOW WHITE-COBALTS: these are the same as the Fallow White Blues except that the body colour is of a pale pinkish cobalt, some of these birds are very pinkish indeed when seen in strong sunlight. There are also Fallow Greywing Cobalts and Fallow White-wing Cobalts. FALLOW WHITE MAUVES: these are the same as the Fallow White Blues and Fallow White Cobalts except that the body colour is of a very soft pale lavender shade: a most pleasing tone. There are also Fallow Greywing Mauves and Fallow White-wing Mauves.

77. ALBINOS (CLEAR WHITE RED-EYES)

These birds are mostly known in the Fancy as Albinos and are clear white throughout not even showing ghost-like markings as mostly seen in Fallow Whites. The beak is a bright orange and the eyes deep red with the feet and legs pink. Albinos are very attractive birds and set off to advantage other colours in a mixed aviary.

78. GREY BLUES

With Grey Blues (Light Greys) the chest, underparts, flanks and rump are an even clear light battleship grey and quite free from any ordinary blue tinting. The markings on nape of neck, shoulders and wings are clear cut black on white and the long tail feathers are dull black. The cheek patches are a light silvery grey and quite distinct from those carried by normal birds and cinnamon birds. GREY COBALTS (medium Greys): these are the same as the Grey Blues except that their body colour is decidedly deeper in shade than the Grey Blue birds. However, this depth of shade varies and it is not possible to tell with any degree of certainty whether the grey is masking blue or cobalt except by the breeding test. GREY MAUVES (dark Greys): these are the same as the Grey Blues and Grey Cobalts except that the body shade is deep grey throughout. It is generally possible to distinguish these birds visibly from the other two Greys. There are also Grey forms of Opaline Blues, Greywing Blues, Cinnamon Blues, Whites, White-wings, Fallow Blues and Pied Blues in all the three shades of each variety.

79. VIOLET BLUES

The Violet Blue birds are practically the same shade of colour as pale Cobalts and it is often they are passed as such. It is not until the violet factor is coupled with the cobalt that the beautiful vivid Violet birds are produced. VIOLET COBALTS: these birds are mostly called just Violets. The chest, underparts, flanks and rump are a wonderful vivid shade of true violet colouring. The nape of neck, shoulders and wings are marked with black undulations on white. The beak is horn coloured, the eyes dark and the feet and legs dull pink or blue. As cobalt is a variable colour so the violet colour carried by these Cobalt birds varies in depth, but all the shades are very beautiful. VIOLET MAUVES: these birds are very similar to the normal Mauves in their general colouring except that it is a deeper tone of mauve and often has actual

violet fleckings on flanks and rump. It must be clearly understood that although there are birds called Violet Blues and Violet
Mauves it is only the Violet Cobalts that actually show clearly
the violet colour. There can be a Violet kind of all the Blue series
such as Opaline Violets, Fallow Violets, Greywing Violets, Cinnamon Violets, Recessive Pied Violets, etc.

80. PIED BLUES

These birds are also called Variegateds, Bi-colours and Harlequins and have quite an unusual arrangement of their colouring.
With all the Pied Blue forms the largest areas of colour are clear
white (like Albinos), the nape of neck, shoulders, wings and tail
are marked by dark ticks or patches of undulations in black,
grey, cinnamon, or ghost markings according to the particular
type to which they belong. A large number of Pied Sky Blues
have the upper part of their chest pure white with an irregular
patch of lustrous blue on the lower part and the rump may be
either clear white or marked with the same blue colour as the
chest. The area of dark feathers can differ with each bird or
groups of birds. Some are almost quite clear, and others three
parts dark and all grades in between. It may be quite possible by
selecting the right birds to produce clear white birds with dark
eyes. The feet and legs are pink and the beak bright orange, with
the eyes dark solid reddish plum coloured without the usual
white iris ring. There can be a Recessive Pied form of all the other
blue and white types as mentioned in the preceding paragraphs.

81. WHITE FLIGHTED BLUES

These birds are somewhat similar in their colour to some Pied
Blues and badly coloured White flighted Blues could easily be
mistaken for true Recessive Pieds by anyone not familiar with
the two kinds. Ideal specimens should have a clear white spot at
the nape of neck with clear white flights and all tail feathers; all
the rest of the body and wings should be dark according to the
colour group to which they belong.

82. YELLOW-FACED BLUES

The Yellow-faced Sky Blues vary quite a lot in their colouring as they can belong to several different types of mutation giving similar colour effect. The most desired exhibition kind has a yellow face (varying from lemon yellow to deep yellow), a patch of yellow markings on wing butts and the light areas of all the tail feathers are yellow. The chest, underparts, flanks and rump are clear sky blue and all the remainder of the body is marked like an ordinary sky blue. The yellow face and body colour gives these birds a unique appearance and there are many breeders who find their production particularly attractive. Another type of the Yellow-faced Blues have a very bright body colour which is a shade mid-way between blue and green and is often called sea green. With these birds there are no white areas at all, the mask, nape of neck, shoulders, wings and tail are yellow in varying degrees of depth. Although quaintly coloured birds these Sea-greens are not outstanding as are the good Yellow-faced Blues with their clear cut lines of colour. YELLOW-FACED COBALTS: these birds are the same as the Yellow-faced Blues except that the body colour is cobalt in one form and a dark bottle green in the other. The yellow faces in some of these Cobalt forms are very deep in colour being almost a golden shade: in fact they were originally known as Golden-faced Cobalts. YELLOW-FACED MAUVES: these birds are the same as the Yellow-faced Blues and Yellow-faced Cobalts except that their body colour is mauve. With one kind the body shade is the usual normal mauve colour and with the other it is a very strange mixture of mauve and ·olive. A most interesting form of these Yellow-faced birds are the Yellow-faced Albinos and with one group of these birds the yellow areas can be very clearly seen against the white. However, with the other kind the white is completely masked by a pale yellowish wash making the birds lemon coloured instead of white. There can be a Yellow-faced form of the Greywing Blues, Cinnamon Blues, White-wing Blues, White-flighted Blues, Fallow Blues, Opaline Blues, Recessive Pied Blues and Violets in all three depths of shade in each type.

83. SLATE BLUES

These birds have a colouring that is about half way between that of the normal Blues and the Grey Blues but of a more warm shade of colour. Their markings, etc., are the same as with the normal birds but they reproduce by a sex-linked manner of inheritance. There can be a Slate form of all the existing types of Blues, Whites, Opalines, Fallows and Pieds.

84. BI-COLOURS (HALF-SIDERS)

These bi-coloured birds are the result of a Chromosome disturbance and the character is therefore not one that can be inherited. Some birds have the line of demarkation straight down the centre of their breast and one complete side of the bird is sky blue and the other light green. These lines are not always equal and some specimens show only small irregular patches of one of the colours. They have appeared and have been noted in the following colour combinations—sky blue and light green, sky blue and cobalt, greywing sky blue and greywing light green, white sky blue and light yellow, dark green and light green, cobalt and dark green, and mauve and dark green. It is quite possible that other bi-coloured birds have appeared at various times but have not been officially reported.

85. FULL BODY COLOURED GREYWINGS

These birds are a combination of the Greywing and Clearwing characters which produce a richly coloured and interesting type of bird. They can be had in both the blue and green forms. The wing markings are usually a little deeper in shade than those of ordinary good Greywings and the body colour is almost the same depth as carried by normal birds but of a very bright colouring. These birds can be bred in several different forms such as Cinnamon, Grey, Opaline, Slate, Fallow and Yellow-faced. Full body coloured Greywings are the only Budgerigars where two different types actually blend and make a new type.

86. OTHER COLOURED VARIETIES

Just prior to the 1939–45 war a race of birds having Plum coloured eyes and a body like dull Greywings were produced and established in several colour shades. Unfortunately they were lost, like the birds having grey markings and yellow or white body colours. By combining the characters of Opalines, Fallows, Greys and Blues in a single specimen, birds having red eyes, dark brown wing markings and a white body can be produced. A similar type but having a yellow body colour has also been produced by the author. In the U.S.A. breeders have evolved birds having clear yellow or clear white bodies with black markings and dark tails. Although established, these attractively coloured birds have not yet been seen in this country. One of the most popular of the newer colours at the present time is the Australian Dominant Pied of which the Banded kind are the most sought after. This mutation occurred in Australia some time during 1935 and it was not until a few years ago that living specimens were imported into this country. Since that time they have made great strides and many beautiful specimens in numerous colours have been and are being produced.

87. CRESTED BUDGERIGARS

A further mutation appeared in North America some time prior to 1939 but this time it was a feather mutation and birds having crests on their heads were raised and established. Examples of this crested kind were imported into this country and it was found that there were three kinds of crests—the flat, round type like the Norwich Crested Canary, the half crest or fringe and the tufted crest. It would appear that the Crested character is a dominant one but its exact method of reproduction is still being investigated. A Specialist Club has been formed to encourage and improve the Crested types. With the help of this Club the Crested birds are now taking their allotted place in aviaries and on the show benches. For some years now they have been a regular feature at the National Exhibition of Cage Birds held in London.

CHAPTER 7

COLOUR BREEDING

88. COLOUR INHERITANCE

THE reproduction of the many different colours and varieties of Budgerigars at first seems to be a very complicated business but if taken simply, from the beginning, it will become quite clear. As with all livestock the various characters they posess (colours and feather patterns in this case) are controlled by minute bodies called Genes whose position on the Chromosomes causes the colours to appear and the study of these matters is called Genetics. In the following paragraphs the broad principles of Genetics as applied to feather colour inheritance in Budgerigars, will be simply and clearly explained.

89. POINTS TO BE OBSERVED

With colour breeding there are several essentials that must always be strictly observed if good and correct results are to be obtained. One is that all breeding pairs must be bred under control whether in cages, pens or aviaries. Another point is that the pedigrees (colours of the parents) of all stock used must be known and recorded. A further point is that all the young ones produced must be ringed with closed metal rings (open metal rings can be used but they are not absolutely safe) and entered in the record book at the time of ringing. Chicks that are not ringed should on no account be moved from one nest to another unless they are first marked on the back with dye, ink or indelible pencil. The same remarks apply to eggs: if they are transferred each egg must be marked and the chicks likewise marked as soon as hatched. Unless the breeder is absolutely sure of the pedigrees of all the stock used, years of working can so easily be wasted.

90. COLOUR GROUPS

Budgerigars can be split into two completely separate groups, those of white ground colour and those of yellow ground colour excluding the Yellow-faced types which are a combination of both.

Yellow ground group	*White ground group*
Green	Sky Blue
Greywing Green	Greywing Blue
Yellow	White Blue
Cinnamon Light Green	Cinnamon Blue
Cinnamon Greywing Green	Cinnamon Greywing Blue
Cinnamon Yellow	Cinnamon White
Slate Green	Slate Blue
Slate Greywing Green	Slate Greywing Blue
Slate Yellow	Slate White Blue
Opaline Green	Opaline Blue
Opaline Greywing Green	Opaline Greywing Blue
Opaline Yellow	Opaline White Blue
Grey Green	Grey Blue
Grey Greywing Green	Grey Greywing Blue
Grey Yellow	Grey White Blue
Fallow Green	Fallow Blue
Fallow Greywing Green	Fallow Greywing Blue
Fallow Yellow	Fallow White Blue
Yellow-wing Green	White-wing Blue
Lutino	Albino
Recessive Pied Green	Recessive Pied Blue
Australian Pied Green	Australian Pied Blue
Violet Green	Violet Blue
Yellow Flighted Green	White Flighted Blue
Lace-wing Yellow	Lace-wing White
(in all 3 depths of shade)	(in all 3 depths of shade)

Colours in the above two groups are called Phenotypes or visible colour types and they in turn can be divided into a very large number of Genotypes for although birds may be visibly one colour they can when mated in certain ways produce other colours. The visible colour of Budgerigars is dependent on the presence in their genetical make-up of certain hereditary factors (Genes) which are positioned on their Chromosomes. It has been proved by countless numbers of different pairings that the colour factors of Budgerigars operate in strict accordance with Mendel's law of heredity.

91. MENDEL'S LAW DISCOVERED

In the early days of Budgerigar colour breeding, the production of the then known colours was rather a matter of chance and a certain amount of inbreeding (breeding with nearly related birds). It was not until 1927 that the principles of Mendel were applied to Budgerigar breeding by Dr. Hans Duncker and Gen. Consul Carl Cremer of Bremen, Germany. These two gentlemen conducted a very large number of experimental pairings, all under strict control and collected a tremendous amount of data which was published both in Germany and in this country. When these articles first appeared they caused quite a lot of controversy amongst the old school of breeders and many lengthy wordy battles took place in the Fancy Press. As the evidence in favour of Mendel's theory mounted, so more and more breeders were convinced of its truth and value and to-day it is an accepted fact with all.

92. DEPTH OF MARKINGS

It is possible to place fairly accurately the depth of markings into five groups—the very dark markings of the Greys (Opalines can also be included because of their deep suffusion), the normal dark markings of the Greens, Blues, Slates and Violets, the intermediate markings of the Greywings, Cinnamons and Fallows, the ghost or light markings of the Yellows, Whites and Clearwings and the complete absence of visible markings of the Albinos, Lutinos and Dark-eyed Clears. The extra deep (grey) markings are Dominant over all other markings, the normal markings are Dominant over intermediate and light, intermediate markings are Dominant over light except in the case of Greywings and Clearwings where the two blend. By examining the above the following conclusions can be agreed: pure Green mated to all other colours (Grey, Violet and sex-linked birds excepted) will give only green coloured young. Pure Greywing mated to Yellow or White will give only Greywing coloured young. All yellow ground birds are Dominant to those belonging to the white ground group. Birds of the same or lighter markings when mated together cannot produce young with darker markings except in the case of the Cinnamons where the sex linkage operates. Both intermediate and lightly marked young cannot be produced from normally coloured birds at the same time, this means that a bird cannot be 'split' for Greywing and White or Yellow at the same time.

93. PURE AND IMPURE BIRDS

Birds of one pure colour paired to birds of the same pure colour always produce pure coloured young unless a rare chance mutation occurs. When two different colours are paired together the resulting young ones will be impure or 'split' birds, taking their visible colour from their Dominant parent. It is the general practice in the Budgerigar Fancy to describe these and all impure birds as 'split' birds such as Light Green 'split' Blue and is written thus, Light Green/Blue, the oblique stroke dividing the bird's visible colour from its hidden hereditary colour characteristics, of which birds can carry several.

94. NORMAL INHERITANCE
RULES
(1) Pure Light Green paired to pure Light Green gives 100% pure Light Green.
(2) Pure Light Green paired to pure Sky Blue gives 100% Light Green /Blue.
(3) Pure Sky Blue paired to Light Green/Blue gives 50% pure Sky Blue and 50% Light Green/Blue.
(4) Light Green/Blue paired to Light Green/Blue gives 25% pure Light Green, 50% Light Green/Blue and 25% pure Sky Blue.
(5) Pure Light Green paired to Light Green/Blue gives 50% pure Light Green and 50% Light Blue.
(6) Pure Sky Blue paired to pure Sky Blue gives 100% pure Sky Blue.

The above Table indicates how the ordinary Light Greens are

Dominant to their Blue counterparts and how the blue colour reappears from certain of the pairings in its pure form. It will be noted in Nos. (4) and (5) that two kinds of green coloured young are produced, the pure and the impure ('split' for Blue). There is no visible way to distinguish between these two kinds of birds, it can only be done by test pairings to Blues. It should be noted that blue coloured birds bred from two Green/Blue parents are equally as pure genetically as those birds which have both parents pure Blue. It will at once be realised that exact percentages are not possible with individual pairs and that this can only be achieved by taking collectively the results of a large number of pairings.

95. HANDING DOWN RECESSIVE CHARACTERS

In paragraph 94 it will be seen that by the pairing (4) and (5) it is possible to produce Green/Blues and not be able to distinguish them visibly from ordinary pure Greens. This being the fact it means that the Recessive blue factor can be handed down from generation to generation and its presence only revealed when suitable matings are made which allows two of the same factors to come together in one bird. Many cases have been recorded where a Light Green strain thought to have been pure had suddenly produced blue coloured chicks. A careful scrutiny of the pedigrees invariably reveals that one of the foundation stock was either a known Green/Blue or a bird of unknown breeding and obviously not a pure Green. Similar instances have occurred in strains of practically every colour and the sudden unexpected appearance of odd colours can be solved by a perusal of the stock recording book.

96. THE CROSSING OF YELLOW WITH BLUE

It has been seen that when the normal Green is paired to Blue all the resulting young are green in colour but 'split' of course for Blue and when mated together will breed Blues, Green/Blues and Greens in the ratio of 1 : 2 : 1. Now if Yellow is used instead of Green to pair to Blue the resulting chicks of the first cross are once again all green in colour. Although they appear to be just the same as the Green/Blues they are definitely different in their genetical make-up and are known in the Fancy under the name of Green/Whites. When two of these Green/Whites are paired together they can breed no less than nine genotypes and amongst them is a new type—the Yellow counterpart of the Blue, i.e., White Blue. The nine different genotypes consists of the following: Greens, Green/Blues, Green/Yellows, Green/Whites, Blues, Blue/Whites, Yellows, Yellow/Whites and White Blues in the ratio of 9 Greens 3 Blues, 3 Yellows and 1 White. The new White type turning up once in every sixteen young. Here again the difference in the Greens, Blues and Yellows can only be ascertained by test pairings.

97. THE DARK FACTOR

The dark factor causes the ordinary light birds of all colours and varieties to appear in two futher depths of shade. This factor operates .in the normal Mendelian way, but controls only the depth of the colour. The rules which operate the dark factor are simple and the same with all birds no matter what colour or variety they may be. For the purpose of simplicity the rules will be shown below, working with the ordinary green coloured birds.

RULES

(1) Light Green (no dark factor) paired to Light Green (no dark factor) gives 100% Light Green (no dark factor).

(2) Light Green (no dark factor) paired to Dark Green (one dark factor) gives 50% Light Green (no dark factor) and 50% Dark Green (one dark factor).

(3) Dark Green (one dark factor) paired to Dark Green (one dark factor) gives 25% Light Green (no dark factor) 50% Dark Green (one dark factor) and 25% Olive Green (two dark factors).

(4) Dark Green (one dark factor) paired to Olive Green (two dark factors) gives 50% Dark Green (one dark factor) and 50% Olive Green (two dark factors).

(5) Light Green (no dark factor) paired to Olive Green (two dark factors) gives 100% Dark Green (one dark factor).

(6) Olive Green (two dark factors) paired to Olive Green (two dark factors) gives 100% Olive Green (two dark factors).

The knowledge of the working of the dark factor is of great use to the breeder particularly when certain intermediate (one dark factor) birds are desired to be produced. For instance, if Cobalts are required the best way to breed all Cobalts (not specially exhibition birds) is to mate Sky Blues to Mauves as per Rule 5 above and only young Cobalts will be raised. The reason for not pairing Cobalts to Cobalts is that they do not breed true to colour as they are impure birds and are governed by Rule 3.

98. BLUE AND THE DARK FACTOR

In the preceding chapter the operation of the dark factor and the Green has been explained and now to deal with the dark and the blue. During the early days of colour breeding it was noticed that certain Dark Green/Blues when paired to Blues produced a large number of Cobalts and only a few Blues and others a large number of Blues and only a few Cobalts. After a considerable amount of research work it was discovered that there existed different breeding kinds of Dark Green/Blue birds which appeared identical to the eye. The cause of this is that in certain matings the dark factor takes up a firm linkage with the blue which results in an excess of Cobalts. This cross over linkage operates with all Dark Green/Blue, Dark Yellow/White, Opaline Dark Green/Blue, Fallow Dark Green/Blue, Cinnamon Dark Green /Blue, etc., etc. One type is known as Type I and when paired to Blues produce 43% blue coloured birds, 7% cobalt coloured birds, 43% dark green coloured birds and 7% light green coloured birds. The other group, the type II, when mated to Blues produce 43% cobalt coloured birds, 7% blue coloured birds, 43% light green coloured birds, 7% dark green coloured birds. type II birds can be bred by pairing cobalt coloured birds (sex immaterial) to Light green/blue coloured birds and numerous other matings where the special hereditary factors are brought together. The value of Type II birds is that they can be used for cobalt breeding in preference to Olive Green/Blues which are invariably smaller birds and produce almost as many Cobalts but of a decidedly better quality and size. Once again it must be clearly stated that there is no visible difference between Type I and Type II birds.

99. THE GREYWING FACTOR

The factor which controls the Greywing depth of colouring is

Recessive to the normal blue and green coloured birds, but is Dominant to the yellow and white kinds. This means that normal birds can and do carry the Greywing factor in a 'split' form, but the Greywing birds cannot be 'split' for normal. Greywings can be 'split' for White and/or Yellow, but White and Yellow birds cannot carry Greywing as a 'split' colour. The Greywings themselves can be divided roughly into two sub-types, those having very dark almost black markings and those with the true pure grey Greywing markings. Darkly marked Greywings can be 'split' for the lightly marked form. In Greywing breeding it is the pure greywinged type that is desired and these birds can only be produced by careful breeding by selected birds. Deeply marked White or Yellow birds although they appear to be lighter than Greywings are not of value to mate to dark Greywings to make the colour lighter. Only the lightly marked Whites and Yellows should be used for Greywing breeding as the deeply marked ones will produce even darker Greywings.

100. THE FALLOW (RED-EYED) FACTORS

As readers have already learned there are distinct breeding forms of the Fallow variety that are practically identical in general colouring. The difference with certain birds is the colouring of the eyes. The name Fallow is derived from a German word meaning uncultivated and describes these birds rather aptly as their colouring is what might well be called unfinished. Most of the Fallows seen to-day are of the original German type and they are Recessive to all the other colours including the Whites and Yellows. It is possible to get a Fallow form of all other colours and varieties and their many combinations. There are numerous Fallow forms which have yet to be bred and others of which only a few odd specimens have so far been produced. An interesting form of the Fallow can be bred by getting together in one bird the Cinnamon, Fallow and White (or Yellow) factors which give the Cinnamon Fallow White (or Yellow). These birds have red eyes and in many instances are pure white or pure yellow throughout and for this reason have been called synthetic Albinos and Lutinos. Not all Cinnamon Fallow Whites and Yellows are pure in colour, some carry faint cinnamon brown tickings on their wing butts and a pale flush of bluish violet on their long tail feathers. Their purity of colour is controlled by the purity of the colour of the stock used in their production. If Cinnamon Fallow Yellow Olives are bred, the yellow colouring is of a lovely deep golden orange shade and most pleasing to the eye. Another interesting member of the group of Fallows is the Opaline Fallow Grey Blue (or Green) where the combination of these factors gives an unusual colour arrangement. These birds have almost clear silvery white or golden yellow body colours with dark brown wing markings and are very handsome indeed. By combining the Violet and Fallow factors in their blue form the author produced birds of a pinkish brown shade hitherto unknown in Budgerigars. Much more experimental work has yet to be done before any real pink or brown coloured birds are bred except of course they arrive by a chance mutation. Another type of Fallow, the English Fallows, which are also Recessive in their manner of reproduction are practically identical to those mentioned above. However, when these different types of red-eyed birds are mated together, all the resulting young ones are normal in colour with black eyes. Each kind of Fallows follow separately the rules given below:

RULES

(1) Pure Fallow paired to pure Normal gives 100% Normal/Fallow.

(2) Pure Fallow paired to Normal/Fallow gives 50% pure Fallow and 50% Normal/Fallow.

(3) Normal/Fallow paired to Normal/Fallow gives 25% pure Normal, 50% Normal/Fallow and 25% pure Fallow.

(4) Normal/Fallow paired to pure Normal gives 50% Normal /Fallow and 50% pure Normal.

(5) Pure Fallow paired to pure Fallow gives 100% pure Fallow.

Once again certain pairings, Nos. (3) and (4) above, give both pure Normals and Normal/Fallows and there is no way to distinguish visibility between them: this can only be done by test pairing to Fallows of the same group.

101. THE DANISH RECESSIVE PIED FACTOR

Until the appearance of the Pied variety all Budgerigar mutations had followed certain fixed patterns of colour and markings. Now, with the Pied character, this is not so and the birds' plumage is broken and does not follow any set line, each bird being a separate individual as to its arrangement of colouring. The Pieds are Recessive like the Fallows and there can be a Pied form of all other colours and varieties. Any coloured bird can carry the Pied character in its 'split' form. As the Pied factor is at present unstable in pattern it may be possible, by carefully selected matings, to produce pure White and pure Yellow birds with dark eyes, also birds where the variegation is evenly distributed. In certain Pied x Normal/Pied pairings a number of the normally coloured birds have been bred which show very small patches of variegation on neck, wings or tail. This seems to indicate that a further variegation character (perhaps local) may be in existence, test pairings are being carried out to try and ascertain the fact. Pied matings of all kinds can be worked out by using the rules for Fallows as shown in paragraph 100 by substituting the word Pied where Fallow appears.

102. THE AUSTRALIAN DOMINANT GREY FACTOR

These birds are known as Greys, Australian Greys and Dominant Greys, but whatever name they are called, they are one and the same variety. The original Dominant Greys, from which sprang all the many types of Grey birds now seen in this country, were imported from Australia where the first mutant was bred. This Grey character is a Dominant one like the Dark factor and being so no birds, whatever colour, can carry Grey in 'split' form. It is possible for birds to have the Grey factor in either single or double quantities without any outward alteration of their plumage, it is only the breeding behaviour which is affected. Greys with single factor, paired to any normal birds will give 50% grey coloured young and those with double factor will give 100% grey coloured young. The Grey factor prevents any blue colouring (cheek patches included) from showing in the plumage and replaces it by a grey colour and this is equally effective in the green as well as the blue groups. As grey only affects the blue colouring it is possible to have three depths of grey in all types because the dark factor is not altered. It is often most difficult to tell visually the difference between Grey Blues and Grey Cobalts, but it is usually possible to distinguish Grey Mauves on account of their extra depth of grey colouring. When describing these birds it is usual to place the Grey first followed by the colour that is being masked, such as Grey Blue, Grey Opaline Light Green, Grey White Mauve, etc. It will clearly be seen that there can be a Dominant Grey form of all other existing colours and varieties. There can even be Grey Albinos and Grey Lutinos although these particular types are almost impossible to tell by sight, nevertheless they do actually exist. Single factor Greys paired to single factor Greys will give the true Mendelian ratio of 25% pure Normals, 50% Greys (single factor) and 25% pure Grey (double factor). There are three matings which will give all grey coloured young, they are Grey (double factor) paired to Grey (double factor), Grey (double factor) paired to Grey (single factor) and Grey (double factor) paired to Normal. The three matings mentioned above operate quite independently of what colour or variety the Grey may actually be masking.

103. THE ENGLISH GREY FACTOR

At approximately the same time as the Grey mutation appeared in Australia another distinct Grey mutation occurred here in this country. This English Grey type although almost identical in its general colouring to the Australian form is Recessive and reproduces in the same way as the Fallows and Pieds. As this is a Recessive variety it means that all other colours and varieties, including the Dominant Grey, could carry this Grey factor in 'split' form. It does not seem that these Recessive Greys are being bred at the moment and they will not be seen at shows or in breeding aviaries. Their existence has been mentioned in case the breeder gets a Grey bird which will not breed any Greys when paired to a Normal.

104. THE SEX-LINKED VARIETIES

At the present time the following varieties—Cinnamons, Opalines, Albinos (and Lutinos) Lace-wings and Slates follow what is known as a sex-linked manner of inheritance. The reason for this sex-control of these characters is that they are situated on the same Chromosome pair that operates the sex of the birds. Sex Chromosomes are the only ones which differ between the two sexes, the others being identical. It is usual to describe the male chromosome pair as XX and the female pair as XY and of course they reproduce 50% of each in the course of breeding operations. The simple diagram on page 61 will show how this works out with the sex-linked varieties. Hen birds give two different kinds of sex factors in their eggs, one X and the other Y, and the cock birds only one kind—X. When the eggs are fertilized the sex of the chicks depends on whether the eggs are of the X kind or the Y kind. If an egg had the Y factor it must definitely be a female and the other member of the Chromosome pair, the X, will carry the factor or factors which will determine the actual colour of the bird. This means that hen birds have only to carry a colour factor on their one X to be that colour whereas cock birds must carry on both. If cock birds have the colour on one X only they are 'split' birds, but hens cannot be 'split' for any sex-linked character. The following rules for sex-linked inheritance should explain the position clearly:

RULES

(1) Sex-linked cock paired to normal hen will give all normal/sex-linked cocks and all sex-linked hens.

(2) Sex-linked hen paired to normal cock will give all normal/sex-linked cocks and all normal hens.

(3) Normal/sex-linked cock paired to sex-linked hen will give sex-linked cocks and hens, normal/sex-linked cocks and normal hens.

(4) Normal/sex-linked cock paired to normal hen will give normal cocks and hens, normal/sex-linked cocks and sex-linked hens.

(5) Sex-linked cock paired to sex-linked hen will give all sex-linked cocks and hens.

These sex-linked rules work out individually for each of the different sex-linked kinds, but when two different kinds are mated together one acts as a normal. For instance, if Lutino sex-linked cocks are paired to Cinnamon hens the results are normal /Lutino Cinnamon cocks and Lutinos hens. The hen birds bred this way are not Lutinos masking Cinnamon, but Lutinos mask-

SEX-LINKED INHERITANCE

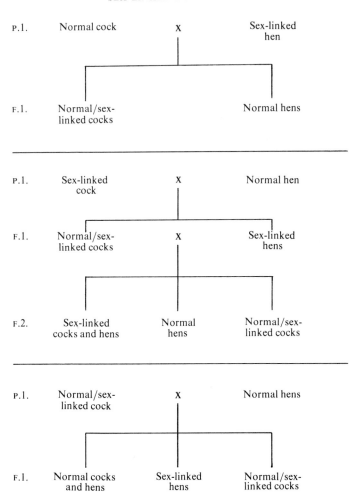

P.1. Normal cock X Sex-linked hen

F.1. Normal/sex-linked cocks Normal hens

P.1. Sex-linked cock X Normal hen

F.1. Normal/sex-linked cocks X Sex-linked hens

F.2. Sex-linked cocks and hens Normal hens Normal/sex-linked cocks

P.1. Normal/sex-linked cock X Normal hens

F.1. Normal cocks and hens Sex-linked hens Normal/sex-linked cocks

ing Normal and the cock birds are 'split' for both Cinnamon and Lutinos. There can be a Lutino (or Albino), Opaline, Cinnamon, Lacewing and Slate form of all the other varieties. With the latter four the different kinds are quite easy to see, but with the Albino and Lutino kinds they are all practically alike to the eye. Nevertheless, there can be an Albino or Lutino form of all other types such as Albino Blue, Albino Grey Cobalt, Albino Opaline Mauve, etc., because an Albino or Lutino must be an Albino or Lutino form of some colour. The only way in which certain Albino Greys and Lutino Greys differ from the ordinary forms is that they are usually devoid of any bluish or greenish reflections which the ordinary birds invariably show when viewed at angles.

105. THE NON SEX-LINKED ALBINOS AND LUTINOS

In addition to the above mentioned sex-linked types of Albinos and Lutinos there also exists a non sex-linked form which reproduced in just the same way as do the other Recessive birds like Fallows. These clear red-eyed birds came into existence approximately at the same time as the sex-linked kind and their advent caused quite a lot of confusion as to the exact way in which clear red-eyed birds reproduce. The two individual kinds are quite alike in their colouring and there can be a non-linked form of all the other types. When, say, non-linked Lutino Light Green cocks are mated to sex-linked Lutino Light Green hens all the resulting young from these clear Yellow red-eyed birds are normally coloured black eyed Light Greens. It is most important that the two different breeding kinds of Albinos and Lutinos should not be crossed with each other as it will have been seen the mixing of these two kinds will cause confusion and especially so in the second generation.

106. THE CLEAR-WING FACTOR

The very beautiful Clearwings or Yellow-wings and White-wings as the two separate colour groups are mostly called, are another form which originated in Australia and were imported into this country. The Clear-wing factor is Dominant to White and Yellow, Recessive to normal, but when coupled with Grey-wing both forms blend together and make a new type; these are called full body coloured Greywings. When pure Clearwings are mated to Yellows or Whites all the resulting chicks are Clearwing in colour but 'split' for Yellow or White. Many of the Clearwings seen at the present time are 'split' for Yellow or White; for this reason especially they should not be mated to Normals in the ordinary way of pairing. Normals paired to Clearwing/White or Yellow give 50% Normal/Clearwing and 50% Normal/Yellow or White and there is no external difference between the two breeding kinds, Normal/Clearwings paired to Whites or Yellows give 50% Normal coloured and 50% Clearwing coloured young. Pure Clearwings paired to pure Greywings give all full body coloured Greywing coloured young, but as so many Clearwings and Greywings are 'split' for Yellow and White the Clearwing x Greywing, mating invariably gives a variety of colours. It is quite an interesting experiment to produce full body coloured Greywings and then cross them back to Yellows or Whites to see the colours reappear. Full body coloured Greywings paired to Yellows or Whites will give 50% Greywing/Yellow or White and 50% Clearwing/Yellow or White. It takes quite a lot of careful selection to breed the real good Clearwings showing the greatest contrast between depth of body colour and absence of colour on wings. To retain that very beautiful bright body shade in Clearwings it is usual to cross Yellowwings with White-wings. It is possible to breed quite a variety of Clearwing forms such as Clearwing Cinnamons, Clearwing Fallows, Clearwing Greys, Clearwing Pieds and of course the very lovely Opaline Clearwings. When the Opaline and Clearwing characters are brought together in one bird the result is most striking. Clearwing Opalines have the brilliant Clearwing body shade and the wings heavily suffused with the same colour after the Opaline pattern. In some instances the Clearwing Opalines are so very heavily suffused all over, that they are called 'Selfs' and very aptly too.

107. THE YELLOW-FACED FACTOR

This character is a most unusual one and produces a whole host of strangely coloured birds, for until the advent of Yellow-faced, white and yellow were not seen on the same birds. There can be Yellow-faced forms of all other varieties in both their Blue and Green groups, but of course the characteristic colouring only shows clearly in the Blue kinds. Breeding experiments have proved that there exist two and possibly three or more kinds of Yellow-faced birds all following a Recessive kind of inheritance. The Yellow-faced factor can be carried by any bird in either single or double quantity. Because some Yellow-faced birds have a deeper yellow colouring than others, it does not mean that they are double factor birds, the actual depth of colouring is no guide to the breeding qualities. One known type of Yellow-faced Blue is called Mutant I and the other Mutant II. When two Mutant I birds are paired they give 25% Normal, 50% Yellow-faced single factor and 25% Yellow-faced double factor. The strange part about these particular double factor birds is that they look just like Normals having no sign of the Yellow face in their plumage. When paired to a Normal all their young are Yellow-faced. Mutant II double factor birds do show the Yellow-face colouring.

108. THE VIOLET FACTOR

In the previous paragraphs two Dominant factors—the dark and the grey have been dealt with and now there is a third one to explain. This one, the Dominant Violet, can *only* be expressed in its real true violet colour when it is combined with a single Dark factor. There can be a Dominant Violet form of all other varieties in both the Green and Blue groups, but it is only the Blue group birds with a single dark factor that will appear to the eye as true violet coloured birds. This variety being a Dominant one makes it *impossible* for any birds, cocks or hens, to carry the factor in 'split' form. It is important to remember when buying Violet factor birds that the birds are either Violets or non-Violets whatever variety they may be. It is quite possible that a further violet form of Recessive nature did exist and still may do so. In the early days of the Violet, its reproduction seemed to be complicated by more than one factor and this matter has never been cleared up satisfactorily. Now to return to the Dominant Violets: there can be both single and double factor birds giving the same visible colour effect. To get the true violet colouring it will be

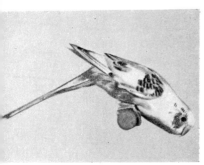 

PLATE V Recessive Pied   PLATE VI Greywing Cobalt.

(*Photos:* Faulkner & Rogers)

PLATE VII. Pair of Sky Blues making friends.

Photo: Walter E. Higham.

PLATE VIII. Two of the first Australian Dominant Pieds
to be bred by the Author.

PLATE IX Flighted control breeding aviaries.

seen that the birds must belong to the Cobalt types to which the Violet factor has been added. The Violet Blues and the Violet Mauves, although they have the Violet factor in their make-up equally as much as the Violet Cobalts, cannot express it with visible clarity. With the Green types the addition of the Violet factor to their make-up gives all of them a distinctive green colouring according to which variety they belong. It is practically impossible to describe these violet green shades on paper, but once seen they are fairly easy to recognize as they are so unlike the usual green colourings. The same rules that apply to the Dark Factors in paragraph 97 can be used to calculate Violet expectations by substituting Violet wherever Dark appears. Violet Cobalts (the Visual Violets) are one of the most attractive of the many coloured types in existence to-day and of these the Opaline White-wing Violet Cobalts are the most brilliant. These lovely birds can be bred from numerous matings and a very suitable one is Opaline Whitewing Mauve hens to White Violet Blue /Opaline cocks. This pairing gives a high proportion of the desired Opaline Whitewing Violet Cobalts.

109. NEW VARIETIES SHOULD BE WATCHED FOR

In the early part of this Chapter quite a wide range of different colour mutations has been explained and their peculiarities dealt with. There have been other mutations in the past which have not been fully established and consequently disappeared again. Mutations are likely to turn up at any time from any pair of birds without the slightest warning and breeders are advised to watch for any variation from the usual amongst their stock. It is quite possible that in the past a number of mutations have passed unnoticed or even if observed have not been investigated. Should anything unusual appear in the nest the breeder should contact someone of wide experience to check the possibilities. It may be possible for the breeder to produce the forerunners of the much sought after Black, Brown or Red Budgerigar! The author will at any time be pleased to advise breeders about any strange coloured bird that they may produce.

CHAPTER 8

TALKING BUDGERIGARS

110. ALL COLOURS MAKE WONDERFUL PETS

It was during the latter part of last century that the first Budgerigars were taught to imitate the human voice and now talking Budgerigars can be seen and heard all over the world—language is no barrier to them! In addition to their ability to talk, Budgerigars can also be trained to do all kinds of tricks and in fact they make the most delightful and endearing little pets. The actual colouring of the birds has no bearing whatsoever on their talking and training ability—Albinos, etc., can be taught equally as well as the ordinary Blues and Greens. There is a fact to be remembered by those who live in large towns and that is to get the more darkly coloured birds as the lighter ones can get their plumage permanently soiled. Cock birds invariably seem to make the best talkers, but hens can also be trained and several outstanding examples of this sex have been noted. It will be realised that all birds are not the same and that the talent of individual birds can vary very considerably even though they may be taken from the same nest.

111. TRAINING TO BE STARTED EARLY

Birds that are to be trained as talking pets should be taken into training as early as possible so that they do not acquire the habits of ordinary aviary kept birds. The best time to take the birds is after they have been out of the nest box for about seven to ten days and are quite independent of their parents for food. It is quite possible to get birds to talk when they are up to six months old, but by that time their capacity to lean the human voice has very much diminished. Young birds are usually much more amenable to handling and it is certainly far easier to gain their complete confidence.

112. THE BEST TRAINERS ARE LADIES

It has been found that ladies, because of the clear pitch of their voices, can train Budgerigars to talk far easier than men. One of the most important items in training is to gain the confidence of all birds being taught. The birds should be approached carefully and unhurriedly at all times during the initial stages and the word or words desired to be leaned should be repeated in a clear slow tone. Simple, short, clear sounding words should always be selected to start teaching the birds as multiple syllable words are rather difficult for them to learn and repeat. Pet birds can be housed in all types of cages and seem to show little or no preference for any particular kind or shape. The feeding of the tame birds is the same as that for the ordinary cage and aviary birds together with a constant supply of grit, cuttlefish bone and clean water. Tit-bits should be given in the form of millet sprays, fruit and fresh green food: sugar, cake and biscuits should be avoided.

113. PET BIRDS CAN BE ALLOWED LIBERTY

If the birds are to be allowed the liberty of the room, the windows and doors must *always* be closed before the cage doors are opened. Open fires should be covered by a guard as the draught created by the chimney can draw birds on to the fire: the author has unfortunately seen this happen several times! All pot plants and flowers should be removed from the room when the pet bird is at liberty as if the green or flowers are eaten by the birds it can cause them harm. Pet birds appreciate play-things in their cages and seem to be very fond of little bells, metal rings, ladders and mirrors. Toys of this kind to be used in the cages of Budgerigars can be bought at all good Bird Accessory shops. It is essential that the cages should be kept always clean and during the warm weather a watch must be kept for red mite which hide in the crevices. A periodical complete cleaning of all parts of the cages will keep red mite in check.

CHAPTER 9

AILMENTS

114. BROKEN LEGS OR WINGS

THE setting of broken bones is not a job that can be done by the ordinary breeder and it is advisable to have any injured birds treated by experts.

115. CHILLS OR COLDS

Budgerigars are prone to getting colds or chills if exposed to draughts or excessive dampness and if not taken in hand at once often ends with serious consequences. Any birds that are noticed to be sitting huddled up on their perches or definitely sneezing should at once be caught and put in a small cage (show type) and brought into a warm even temperature. Warmth has a wonderful reviving effect on all sick birds and if given in time the majority of the patients will be completely recovered in a few days. When the sick birds are fit again care must be taken to see that they are well hardened off before they are returned to their cages or aviaries.

116. CUTS AND WOUNDS

Occasionally birds will be bitten by others or get some of their body cut on exposed wire ends, causing freely bleeding wounds. Should this happen the birds must be caged and kept quiet for a few days, the wounds being cleaned with a good antiseptic. Budgerigars heal very quickly and clean healthy wounds are usually quite healed in a week or ten days.

117. EGG BINDING

Egg binding of course only affects hen birds and only then when they are weakly, over fat, too young for breeding or get chilled just prior to laying. An egg-bound hen is usually quite easy to spot as she will sit huddled up on the nest box perch or in a corner on the floor of the cage or aviary. The sick bird should at once be taken into a warm even temperature and the vent oiled with a little sweet or olive oil applied with a small brush. Usually the hen will pass the egg within a few hours of being brought into the heat. If this does not cause her to lay she can be steamed over a jug of hot water for a few moments at a time, this will usually cause her to pass the egg.

118. FITS

Budgerigars are excitable little birds and at the commencement of the breeding season an odd bird or so may have a fit or seizure. Sometimes this happens so quickly that the breeder has no time to do anything and the bird dies immediately. In other cases birds will be seen to flutter to the ground and behave in a strange manner, such birds should be caged and kept quiet for a few days feeding them on plain canary seed, a little green food and fresh water.

119. FRENCH MOULT

The complete cause of French Moult (the dropping of partly developed feathers in young birds) has yet to be discovered, there are many theories on the subject all of which fit certain cases. Birds that are very badly affected and leave their nest boxes almost denuded of feathers should be destroyed at once. The majority of affected birds however only drop flight or tail feathers and these mostly grow again in due course. It is quite a good plan to bathe the wings and tail in a solution of T.C.P., Dettol or something similar, before the feathers start to grow again. Birds that have had French Moult make ideal pets, but should *not* be used in the breeding quarters.

120. SCALY FACE

Scaly face is not an actual disease, but a condition brought about by minute insects which attack beak ceres, skin surrounding the eyes and the feet and legs, giving them a rough scaly appearance. Scaly face is very infectious and one affected bird can quickly infect all others in the same cage or aviary. It is most fortunate that scaly face can easily be permanently cured by the simple method of painting the affected parts with one of the advertised patent cures or with T.C.P., Dettol, or some similar germicide. The cages and aviaries where infected birds have been housed should be thoroughly disinfected before being used again.

121. In case the above paragraphs sound too alarming let it be said that generally speaking Budgerigars are extremely healthy and vigorous birds and only a very small percentage of them actually get sick. Budgerigars have been known to live to the age of twenty-two, but the normal span of pet birds is between seven and nine years, with breeding birds a year or two less.

CHAPTER 10

EXAMPLES OF THEORETICAL EXPECTATIONS

122. SELECTED EXAMPLES

IN the following theoretical matings the colours have been selected from the many varieties to give the reader an idea of what to expect when certain birds are paired together. With individual matings the percentages of the different colours vary from one extreme to the other, the actual percentages are worked out over many matings. For this reason the percentages have been omitted from the pairings. If these expectations are used in conjunction with the various sets of Rules, the breeder can work out the results of all other pairings.

MATING	EXPECTATIONS
Blue x Light Green/Blue	Blue. Light Green/Blue.
Light Yellow x Olive Green	Dark Green/Yellow.
White Blue x Greywing Green/White	Greywing Green/White. Greywing Blue/White. Light Yellow/White. White Blue.
White Cobalt x Dark Yellow/White	Light Yellow/White. Dark Yellow/White. Olive Yellow/White. White Blue. White Cobalt. White Mauve.
Opaline Blue cock x Light Green/Blue hen	Light Green/Opaline Blue cocks. Blue/Opaline cocks. Opaline Light Green/Blue hens. Opaline Blue hens.

71

MATING	EXPECTATIONS
Opaline Whitewing Blue cock x White Cobalt hen	Whitewing Cobalt/Opaline White cocks. Whitewing Blue/Opaline White cocks. Opaline Whitewing Blue/White hens. Opaline Whitewing Cobalt/ White hens.
Fallow Dark Green/Blue x Blue/Fallow	Light Green/Fallow Blue. Blue/Fallow. Fallow Light Green/Blue. Fallow Blue.
Fallow Light Yellow /White x Blue/Fallow White	Light Yellow/Fallow. White Blue/Fallow. White Blue/Fallow. Blue/Fallow White. Green/Fallow White. Fallow Light Yellow. Fallow White Blue. Fallow Blue/White. Fallow Green/White.
Whitewing Blue/White x Light Yellow/White	White Blue. Light Yellow/White. Whitewing Blue/White. Yellow-wing Green/White.
Whitewing Mauve/White x White Violet Blue	Whitewing Violet Cobalt. White Violet Cobalt.
Lutino Green/Blue cock x Blue hen	Lutino Green/Blue hens. Albino Blue hens. Green/Albino Blue cocks. Blue/Albino cocks.

MATING	EXPECTATIONS
White Blue cock x Lutino Light Yellow/White hen	White Blue hens. Light Yellow/White hens. White Blue/Albino cocks. Light Yellow/Albino cocks.
Opaline Cobalt cock x Light Green/Blue hen	Blue/Opaline cocks. Cobalt/Opaline cocks. Light Green/Opaline Blue cocks. Dark Green/Opaline Blue cocks. Opaline Blue hens. Opaline Cobalt hens. Opaline Light Green/Blue hens. Opaline Dark Green/Blue hens.
Pied Mauve x Light Green /Pied Blue	Pied Cobalt. Pied Dark Green/Blue. Cobalt/Pied. Dark Green/Pied Blue.
Pied Light Yellow/White x Greywing Blue/Pied	Greywing Green/Pied White. Greywing Blue/Pied White. Pied Greywing Green/White. Pied Greywing Blue/White.
Grey Blue/Blue x Light Green/Blue	Grey Blue/Blue. Grey Light Green/Blue. Blue. Light Green/Blue.
Grey Olive Green/Blue x Blue	Grey Dark Green/Blue. Grey Cobalt/Blue. Dark Green/Blue. Cobalt.
Lace-wing Yellow cock x Light Green hen	Normal/Lace-wing cocks. Lace-wing hens.
Normal/Lace-wing cock x Light Green hen	Normal/Lace-wing cocks. Normal cocks and hens. Lace-wing Yellow hens.

CHAPTER 11

EXHIBITING

123. EXHIBITING

In the previous Chapters, the housing, breeding and general management of Budgerigars have been dealt with and it remains now to discuss the exhibiting side of the Fancy. Without a doubt Budgerigars are the most popular of all caged birds and a glance into any exhibition will invariably show them to be the largest single section on view. Budgerigars have much to recommend them as show birds: they take kindly to cage life; they are reasonably easy to train; they travel by rail, air or road and they are to be had in such a wonderful range of beautifully coloured varieties. It is quite a good thing to exhibit home-bred stock against those birds of other breeders as it stimulates enthusiasm and definitely helps in maintaining and improving the general qualities of the breed.

As it will be realised there is far more to exhibiting Budgerigars, or any birds, than just catching them up from an aviary, putting them into a show cage and sending them along to an exhibition. Quite a lot of training and preparation are needed before the birds are in a suitable state for going to a show. In the following paragraphs the reader will find the method by which birds are brought to the desired show excellence.

124. PRIZE WINNING STANDARDS

There are certain qualities which birds must possess before they can gain prizes in competition on the show bench: firstly, perfect bodily condition with no missing feathers or claws: secondly, they must be near to the recognized standard of perfection and of the correct colouring required by the individual variety and lastly they must be perfectly quiet and steady and quite at home in a show cage. It is not enough for birds to have one or two of these good qualities, they must have a *balanced* combina-

74

tion of them *all* to be really successful exhibition birds.

125. GENERAL DESCRIPTION

Below is a general description of the points desired in exhibition birds. The head should be broad and well rounded and not pinched at the front, flat on top or cut away at the back, with the eyes clear and well set. The neck and back should be nicely filled, rounded and free from hollows or lumpiness. The mask should be deep, clear and ornamented with four clean, well-placed round spots (when the variety carries spots). Actually the birds have six spots, three on each side, but the third ones are usually almost obscured by the cheek patches; multiplicity of spots is a definite failing. The chest and underparts should be full with a good clean sweep to the tail which is carried in line with the body. The wings should be nicely braced, neither too short or too long and carried in line with the tail. The birds should stand well and clear on their perches in a bold, upright position and must be perfectly balanced throughout. Unless a bird is well balanced it cannot be a really first class show bird as it must be stressed again, one or two good points will not make it a winner.

126. PREPARING YOUNG BIRDS FOR SHOW

It is rather important that birds intended for exhibition should receive primary training in that field during the early stages of their lives; this first training usually consists of getting the young birds thoroughly used to going in and out of show cages and being moved from place to place. The breeding cages as shown in Fig. 1 can be used as stock training cages and show cages can be hung over the open wire doors and the birds allowed free access. By putting tit-bits of green or millet sprays into the show cages their use will be greatly encouraged. It is surprising how very quickly young birds will get thoroughly at home in show cages and will enter them quite fearlessly. Once the young birds are fully accustomed to show cages they can be allowed to moult in their stock cages, pens or aviaries with just an occasional run in a show cage until they have got their full adult plumage and then more serious training commences. Special classes are put on at most shows for birds of the year that are wearing a closed metal ring bearing identification markings and the year clearly stamped.

127. SHOW CONDITION

However perfect in colour and shape birds may be, they will not win at competitive shows unless they are in real first class show condition. With fully adult birds show condition means that they are in perfect health and all feathers complete, unbroken and of fine texture and with a shining finish. Birds are brought into show condition by correct feeding, good clean housing and periodical spraying. Feeding on a diet that is too fattening will soon spoil the desired clear-cut outline with pads of surplus fat. A good standard seed mixture for exhibition birds is two parts large canary, two parts small canary, half part Indian millet and half part white millet. Groats and oats are best left out of the diet as these are definitely of a fattening nature as also is too much white millet. Care must be taken when giving green food to see that it is not of a too juicy kind that can soil the feathers, particularly round the face. Clean water, grit and cuttlefish bone must *always* be available in the stock cages. Clean coarse pine sawdust on the floors of the stock cages will ensure that the birds do not get their flights and tails soiled by droppings. As Budgerigars are not regular bathers they should be sprayed periodically with clean filtered rain water or tap water that has been boiled. All spraying should be done early in the day so that the bird's feathers are quite dry before roosting time. Birds should only be shown in clean cages of the standard design with the floor covered by seed.

128. ENTERING BIRDS AT SHOWS

The new exhibitor should read most carefully the show rules and the schedule of classes before the entry forms (these are provided by the show promoting society) are filled up. If any doubt arises as to the correct class in which a particular bird should be entered, advice can be sought from the show secretary or members of the show committee. These names appear in the schedule. When the entry forms are completed they should be sent well before the advertised closing date together with all necessary fees to the show secretary. The rail labels for the outside of the travelling cases should be securely fixed in place with strong drawing pins and the under sides of the labels filled in clearly with the owner's name and address, and fixed to the lid of the case. Rail fares must be paid for both outward and return journeys when the birds are despatched. It should be ascertained from the nearest railway station the time of the train that will get the birds to their destination well in time for staging and before the judging is scheduled to start. When the birds return from a show they should be put back into their stock cages and given water, food and tit-bit. The show cages should be cleaned and washed if necessary and replaced in the travelling case ready for use. A visit to a cage bird exhibition will be of great value to the intending exhibitor as it will indicate what is necessary to make successful exhibition birds. The new exhibitor must not be disheartened by failing to gain awards in the first attempts at showing, but should see why the other birds were in front and endeavour to reverse the placings another time either by showing better birds or birds in better show condition. It is the spirit of competition that keeps the bird breeders right on their toes whether it is at exhibitions or in the field of experimental colour breeding.